Wine, *Women* & WEALTH

Inspirational Stories of Women
Who Got Their Financial Act Together —
and How You Can Too.

by Denise Arand

BALBOA.PRESS
A DIVISION OF HAY HOUSE

D1016662

Balboa Press books may be ordered through booksellers or by contacting:

Balboa Press
A Division of Hay House
1663 Liberty Drive
Bloomington, IN 47403
www.balboapress.com
1 (877) 407-4847

Because of the dynamic nature of the Internet, any web addresses or links contained in this book may have changed since publication and may no longer be valid. The views expressed in this work are solely those of the author and do not necessarily reflect the views of the publisher, and the publisher hereby disclaims any responsibility for them.

The author of this book does not dispense medical advice or prescribe the use of any technique as a form of treatment for physical, emotional, or medical problems without the advice of a physician, either directly or indirectly. The intent of the author is only to offer information of a general nature to help you in your quest for emotional and spiritual well-being. In the event you use any of the information in this book for yourself, which is your constitutional right, the author and the publisher assume no responsibility for your actions.

Any people depicted in stock imagery provided by Getty Images are models, and such images are being used for illustrative purposes only. Certain stock imagery © Getty Images.

Print information available on the last page.

ISBN: 978-1-9822-3638-0 (sc)
ISBN: 978-1-9822-3637-3 (hc)
ISBN: 978-1-9822-3639-7 (e)

Library of Congress Control Number: 2019915772

Balboa Press rev. date: 10/25/2019

Dedication

To the strong woman who made me who I am:
My mom, Kay Trimm

To the strong women who love and encourage me always:
My daughters, Elizabeth Hansen & Suzanne McDonnell

The strong soon-to-be women who
inspire me to make this a better world:
My granddaughters, Molly and Grace Hansen

Contents

Foreword

When I first heard from Denise Arand about her idea to write a book about Wine, Women and Wealth, I reflected back to 2004, when I had a "chance" opportunity to see Marti Barletta speak at a conference about marketing to women. Barletta is one of the world's foremost authorities on this subject and has written several best-selling books of her own regarding this phenomenon. As she spoke about the role women will play in the massive change occurring in commerce and our economy, I was struck by the opportunity this could present in the financial services. For seemingly 250 years, the financial industry blueprint would probably be best labeled as a "good ol' boys" club because men dominated the entire structure, from agent to executive levels.

But, how to capture and grow this incredible and unique opportunity evaded me … until Denise arrived at our company. With a passion to engage, educate, and empower women in their financial lives, Denise created the Wine, Women and Wealth program. This fantastic social networking and educational workshop has literally revolutionized our company and the lives of thousands of women throughout the United States. Denise's enthusiastic commitment to this revolution spread like wildfire throughout our company, and she has since duplicated herself through many incredible female leaders nationwide.

At the time our company embraced Denise's ideas, we looked very much like the rest of the traditional, male-dominated insurance industry. At the writing of this book, after years of dedication to this crusade by Denise and our female partners, I am proud to say that Five Rings Financial is currently a little more than 60 percent female, from agents to administration and executives—including Denise, a Partner in our firm and one of our Executive Vice Presidents. This dedication to educating and empowering women in their financial lives through Wine, Women and Wealth is a phenomenon of its own, and it has enabled our company to continue to grow at a 30–40 percent increase every single year since inception. We owe Denise and all of our other female leaders a huge debt of gratitude for creating such a revolutionary, paradigm-changing event.

Proof of the program's significance is the number of imitators (and trademark and copyright infringers) that have attempted to duplicate Denise's program. They are right in recognizing the opportunity, the need, and the impact. However, Wine, Women and Wealth alone does not work; it's just a program. What are required are the "spirit" and the "passion" and the "love" that Denise and our female leaders invest into the lives of their guests and their clients. I believe you will recognize this magic ingredient in the stories shared in this book. I hope you enjoy it as much as I enjoy getting to hitch a ride along with the fantastic women of our company as they revolutionize financial literacy for women.

Mike Wilk
President and CEO,
Five Rings Financial, Inc.

Introduction

This book is for you. I wrote it with the intention to create a place of inspiration and reference for women who want more success in their relationship with money. And I'm talking about all women: paycheck-to-paycheck women; wealthy women; self-made women; just-trying-to-figure-themselves-out women; trust fund women; women who have made money and lost it - and those women who've made it back again. Married women, single women, divorced women, and widowed women. Young women just starting out in life, career women at the top of the corporate ladder, entrepreneur women, moms driving the crazy carpool schedule, and women facing retirement.

You see, money can be a rather charged topic in our world, especially if you live in the United States in the twenty-first century. Money is simply a tool that we use in exchange for things that we want. But we've made-up so many stories about it, giving money its own life and personality, that we don't see it for what it is: a means to get what we want in life. In addition, we've made up a lot of stories about getting what we want in life: that it's bad to want to have money, that we're selfish, that we're greedy, not worthy, or not deserving. But that's just the story many of us tell ourselves about money! Ultimately, it's not how much money you have or don't have—it's how you deal with it. We've all gone to school for so many years and learned all about reading, writing, and arithmetic, but we never *ever* learned about how money really works. Especially as women. And unless you had a family that was a great example to follow, once you're an adult, you are on your own.

Here's the challenge with that. In "polite" society, it's taboo to talk about money – right up there with sex, religion, and politics. Which means that money is _not_ talked about at cocktail parties, it's _not_ talked about around the dinner table, it's _not_ talked about in the classroom - or anywhere else for that matter! While some people have an innate knack for dealing with money, most just simply do the best they can, make mistakes along the way, and manage to get by. Imagine about how great life would be if you knew the money rules ahead of time, and if you knew what tools you could use to create greater financial success! Financial fads come and go; financial principles are locked in stone. Knowing financial principles and knowing what is _always_ true about money will help you win the money game in the long run.

A few years ago, working as a financial professional, I realized that a lot of women have had little, if any, education about money. On top of that, most women have little confidence and little involvement with the money that they have: married women who have given much of their financial control over to their husbands (Really? In this day and age?!), single women who have just put their heads in the sand and let the chips fall where they may, widowed women who have decided they would just spend all of their money to ease their grief. That, along with the fact that women have been pretty much invisible to the financial industry, was creating a financial disaster! In 2007, the US Department of Labor Statistics reported that 90 percent of women will have sole control of their money at some point in their lives, yet 72 percent of them are completely unprepared for this. That frightening statistic began my journey of educating and empowering women about money.

I was (and am) fortunate to work for an amazing company, Five Rings Financial, where I was encouraged to pursue the idea of creating a women's social and educational workshop. This event would be designed to educate women about their relationship with money in a relaxed environment and build a community of women who support one another as they strive for more financial success. There would be no sales pitch; it was a purely educational and social event. The president and founder of Five Rings Financial, Mike Wilk, had followed the work of Marti Barletta, known as the First Lady of Marketing to Women, and had realized the importance of working with women in the financial sector. When I brought this idea to Mike, he fully endorsed me to beta test it in my area.

I begin formulating a plan as to how this women's event would work. I had just moved back to California from Colorado, and although I was back in my home state, I was in San Diego, not in the LA beach cities where I'd grown up. I didn't know anybody except my dog, my brother-in-law, and my husband—all male. I needed some girlfriends! I had awesome financial information to share! And I love wine! That was the thought process that launched Wine, Women and Wealth.

Wine, Women and Wealth began with four new girlfriends in Carlsbad, California, at a tiny wine bar near the beach. We had originally met at a networking group about a month earlier, and we clicked right away! They were all entrepreneurs and wanted to know more about how they could create more financial success in their lives. They wished to build a nest egg as a safety net for the present, create retirement income for later, and eventually pass on a legacy for their families. They were looking for protection against that "what ifs" in life—things like illness, economic downturns, family emergencies, and the big bad daddy of them all, taxes. I knew I had all of the tools to help them, if I could only teach them. That first meeting was amazing, and little did I know the impact that Wine, Women and Wealth would have on so many women over time. The five of us left feeling empowered and happy to have begun a conversation about money and to have started building a community of women on their way to more financial success. We promised to get together in one month, invite a few more girlfriends, and support one another not only in business but life in general.

What happened next was amazing! A year later, I shared the concept of Wine, Women and Wealth with the other female leaders of Five Rings Financial. One of the unique things about our company is that we are a financial services company with a predominantly female field force. That's pretty fantastic when you consider that the world of financial professionals has been, and continues to be, overwhelmingly male! Our female leaders loved the idea of creating Wine, Women and Wealth in their own communities, bringing education, inspiration, and financial success to women across the country.

As time went on and we hosted more and more events, I came to realize that there were certain ideas that stop women from being successful with money such as:

- Old trains of thought:
  "I am not good with money." or
  "I am a woman, therefore I don't
  understand numbers."
- Societal beliefs:
  "Money doesn't grow on trees." or
  "Money is the root of all evil."

- Family and cultural attitudes:

> "Marry a good man, like a doctor, and you won't
> have to worry about money." or
> "My family struggled with money,
> so I am not worthy of having financial success."

...to name a few. For many women, talking about how money
works would do no good until they got their heads around their
relationship with money. Instead of focusing on the next best
investment or retirement savings plan, we focused more on
how women deal with money and how to overcome some of the
obstacles they face that block financial success.

One of my favorite outcomes from Wine, Women and Wealth
is the relationships I've built with the women I've met at the
communities we have created all over the country. It's pretty
amazing what happens when women gather together to create
something positive not only in their own lives but in the lives of
others. Women are collaborative creatures by nature; we want to
help, to share. At our events, our attendees have found new clients, new strategic partners, new travel buddies, new OB/GYNs
(that really happened!), new mentors ... even new best friends.
This happens because our community is open and welcoming –
we encourage one another to share new ideas, to talk about what
matters to us, and we encourage each woman to tell her story.
I realized as time went on that everyone has a story, and sometimes someone else's story is a lot like yours. If you can use these
stories as a stepping-stone, as a way to inspire yourself to more
success, then this book is for you.

In the chapters that follow, you will learn the stories of the
women of Wine, Women and Wealth. Amazing women who
overcame obstacles, both big and small, to find a happier place
in life and a better relationship with money. What is so inspirational is that they learned the concepts, took action and applied

those concepts in their own lives, and became more financially successful. While the women you'll meet in these pages are all real women, and their chapters are all based on their financial stories, most of their names and some of the details of their lives have been changed to protect their privacy.

You'll also meet some of my Wine, Women and Wealth "Sisters" - Five Rings Financial agents who also host our events. I am blessed to work with the most amazing women! As I began to write this book, I realized that I didn't have a corner on all of the inspirational stories about women financially transforming their lives. I knew I had to ask some of the remarkable ladies who host our events in their communities to write about the women they know who have experienced a 'financial makeover' and are now thriving. The response was overwhelming! Each and every contributor was excited to share a story that could help another woman 'get her financial act together'. You'll find each author's bio is included at the end of each of the chapters she penned.

We all have that go-to girlfriend who always has the right thing to say when we are having relationship issues, or a bestie who has awesome parenting advice and, of course the one who will tell you the truth about whether that bathing suit looks good on you, right? We want to be your go-to girlfriends about improving your finances and relationship with money.

Tamra
"I Want to Be Smart with My Money"

by Mara Simoneau

When I first met Tamra, she was in her early thirties, dating a great guy, enjoying her career as a trademark attorney, and making good money. She found out about our Wine, Women and Wealth community in Colorado on the internet—thank goodness for Google! Tamra was looking for community. She wanted to meet like-minded women and find other successful female professionals to hang out with, and girl, did she ever! After attending a few events and making awesome connections, Tamra approached me at the end of an evening event and asked what she needed to do to sit down and find out more about what we do. As millennials, we both whipped out our Google calendars and booked a video chat on the spot—gotta love technology!

During our first video chat, Tamra explained her situation. "Mara, I make great money. I save money. I own a home. I feel like I'm on the right track, but I've never felt like I had someone who could help me make sure that was true. I feel like Wine, Women and Wealth was the perfect opportunity for me to get to know you, and I'm so glad you weren't pushy!" Then she gave a you-have-no-idea-how-true-that-statement-is laugh, apparently based on some past experience.

She went on to say:

> In my twenties, I worked as a paralegal while I was
> finalizing my degree. I was offered a 401(k), so I took
> advantage of that and max-funded it. I figured I'd
> better start saving now. Between my contributions
> and the matching, I saved about forty thousand dol-
> lars. Then I left that job and started working at a new
> firm after passing the bar. I simply left that old 401(k)
> there because I didn't know what to do with it.
>
> Now that I'm at my new job, I'm in charge of my own
> client acquisition, and it's almost like I'm self-em-
> ployed. I have a great salary with bonuses, but I don't
> have a traditional retirement plan offered at work. I'm
> wondering what I should do with my money to make
> sure I keep saving and moving in the right direction
> toward retirement. I've funded a Roth IRA in the past,
> but that just doesn't feel like I'm saving enough. I
> know if I want to enjoy my later years, I need to start
> thinking about all of this stuff as soon as possible.
>
> If I could find the right place to save my money,
> I'd like to be saving around one thousand dollars a
> month, plus I want to do something with that old
> 401(k). Also, I know you mentioned living benefits
> in one of your presentations at Wine, Women and
> Wealth, and that intrigues me as well.
>
> I also think it's important that I share with you that
> although I save money, I still don't feel like I have a
> great relationship with money. I thought it was so
> interesting that you shared that concept at Wine,
> Women and Wealth. I'd never thought about it until
> then. As I reflect on my upbringing and my parents'

habits, I realize that my parents always provided for me, but they didn't really know how to teach me about money because they were never taught about money. I saw them struggle financially, and I guess that's why I'm such a saver: I want a different life. However, I feel like even though I'm saving, I'm not sure I'm going to reach my goals. I think I need help setting those financial goals, so I know that I'm on track. I'm hoping you can help me with my money self-talk as we go through this process.

Tamra and I chatted further about her goals, her love of travel, and her potential promotion at work. She said one of the firm partners really loved her style and had been giving her more responsibility; based on that, she was going to ask for a raise this week.

Then she redirected the conversation and asked me more about what our accounts and instruments looked like. I drew her a few pictures and explained how indexed accounts work. "When a stock index, like the S&P 500, goes up, our accounts go up with it up to the cap. When a stock index goes down, our accounts go sideways. In other words, you never lose your money!" Just like all of my clients, she said that it sounded too good to be true, and of course I agreed because I'd felt the same way the first time my mentor had drawn me this picture. But then I showed her how it's not too good to be true; it's just good business. It's a way that the companies we represent create a win-win for themselves and their clients.

I drew one more picture, recapping living benefits and how cool it is to be able to access money from a life insurance policy in case of a terminal, critical, or chronic illness—life insurance you don't have to die to use. This is a game changer for people who never thought they needed life insurance. In the old days, you only bought life insurance if you wanted to leave money to a loved one. Today, life insurance with living benefits gives you access to a pool of money in case you are ever diagnosed with a serious illness or have a severe accident. It covers us for the stuff that we never plan for! Tamra shared with me that she had a friend in her early thirties who had recently been diagnosed with thyroid cancer, adding that it was a wake-up call for both of them!

As we wrapped up our video chat, we laughed about retirement and how different our view of it was from our grandparents'. We talked about how much we both loved what we do for a living and decided that planning for retirement was more like planning for future flexibility to travel and always pursue what we love. After toasting our virtual coffee, we scheduled our next video chat and wrapped up our session.

Based on everything Tamra had shared with me, I got to work running illustrations and projections for her future money. This is one of the coolest parts about what I get to do because I can share with my clients a bright vision for their financial futures. I crunched numbers for her 401(k) rollover, her monthly savings goals, and her living benefits needs. Everything came together, creating an awesome plan that would allow her to have more than enough for retirement and enough living benefits that she'd never have to worry about finances if she experienced an unexpected negative life event. I was so excited to share the scenarios with her! I could hardly wait! Luckily, our next meeting was the following day.

Every time I have a second chat with a client, I start out by asking whether she or he has thought of any questions since our last conversation. This gives my client a chance to ask anything that has come up from internet research or chatting with family or friends. So many people are fascinated by indexed accounts and living benefits that they often share the concepts with the people they love most. Tamra had a few questions that she wanted clarified about how indexed *accounts* are different from indexed *mutual funds*. I explained that while indexed mutual funds are tied to the stock market in both the up and down direction, indexed accounts can only go up to the cap or sideways; they can't ever drop if the stock market takes a dip. She loved that!

Those were her only questions, so it was time for the best part— the numbers! I have a really simple way of showing how the numbers project into a client's future, summarizing potential income at ages sixty and seventy. Tamra was amazed at what her 401(k) would turn into simply by using indexed compound interest and being protected from the downside. She wasn't going to add any more money to this account, but it was going to grow significantly over her working years. Then I showed her the projected growth of the monthly savings plan she wanted to start. A thousand dollars per month, starting now, was going to make her a very wealthy woman, and the best part was she would be able to access this portion of her money tax free by utilizing a little-known, tax-free strategy. Lastly, she could not believe how much coverage she could get for living benefits with just a small monthly cost. As we worked through each piece of this comprehensive plan, I answered every question she had along the way.

Once we were done, she said, "Awesome! What do I need to do to get this started? I want it all!" I'm used to getting this response from my clients, but each time it's still a thrill. I love that what I have to offer makes so much sense that I never have to use sales tactics or pressure. My clients decide what is good for them based on the information I've shared. It's the very best way to work. We set up all of her accounts, and I helped her facilitate the rollover, completed paperwork for her, and walked her through every step. Tamra was amazed at how simple the process was and said that she actually enjoyed it. What a bonus!

When all her new accounts were complete, we went to lunch to celebrate! Of course, we chatted about everything from pets to food to travel, and in the end, she thanked me and gave me a huge hug. Tamra and I were excited to start this journey together, and I was grateful that she trusted me enough to educate her and walk her through this process. As we wrapped up our lunch, I invited her to come back to Money 101 (another educational workshop Five Rings Financial offers) and Wine, Women and Wealth as often as she'd like. I told her she was always welcome to bring friends who might enjoy our education and community. She thanked me from the bottom of her heart for supporting her in getting on track financially, both with her money and her mind-set.

MARA SIMONEAU

"I love telling Tamra's story because that's the magic of what I get to do every day: meet amazing women, connect with them where they're at, guide them along the path with an educational process, and help them make great decisions with their money. I'm blessed to get to do what I love with clients I care about and enjoy hanging out with! It doesn't get better than that—I call it "Life Made to Order"!

A Little about Mara

Mara is changing the money conversation for good! Armed with a feisty attitude and a no-nonsense approach to finances, this cool, quirky, and colorful blonde brings a fresh approach to the oh-so-taboo subject of money. She is on a mission to empower Americans to gain financial literacy, confront their fears, and move forward in life with a plan that works. As an Executive Vice President of Five Rings Financial, Mara is passionate about empowering women and entrepreneurs to find fulfillment and financial freedom on their terms. With her experience as an entrepreneur in diverse industries, she brings her understanding of what it takes to own a business and plan for the future.

When Mara learned about the power of the products available through Five Rings Financial, she knew she had found her dream career. Her clients don't have to risk their money to get great upside potential; she calls it the S.W.A.N. (Sleep Well At Night) Plan! During her career, she's also gained a passion for empowering women to embrace a "New Money Soundtrack", changing their money stories and their financial futures! Mara has helped launch Wine, Women and Wealth communities nationally and loves guiding new women to successful careers in financial services.

In her personal life, Mara is an avid traveler, venturing to all seven continents before her thirtieth birthday, visiting more than forty countries and counting! She's a stepmother to four teenagers, a doggy momma to three rescue pups, a snowboarder, a lover of business development, a mentor to women nation-wide, and a big fan of life. Mara and her husband, Andre, are a dynamic duo at home and in business, and they are thrilled to have created their Life Made to Order, together! They look for the love, blessings, learning, and adventure in every single day!

Latisha
A Woman of Action

by Erica Moore

I had the pleasure of meeting Latisha when she was invited to Wine, Women and Wealth by a coworker in 2014. Latisha was thirty-four at the time and was a single, never-married professional woman who had been working as a contractor for the federal government for several years. She had a quiet, warm presence, just a pleasant person to be around. Latisha enjoyed the event and began regularly attending Wine, Women and Wealth.

At the end of each Wine, Women and Wealth event, I always offer attendees the opportunity to have a private meeting with one of our Five Rings Financial agents. Women often want to talk one-on-one to discuss topics they may not feel comfortable sharing in a group setting. After one of the events, Latisha pulled me aside and asked if I would be willing to meet with her. She explained that she'd wanted to ask for a meeting for a while, but she was embarrassed about her financial situation and wasn't sure I would be able to help her anyway. She said, "My finances are such a mess, I think I'm beyond help." Sadly, many women believe their financial situations are beyond help, so they don't even ask. I reminded her that Five Rings agents operate in a no-judgment zone. I told her I would do my best to help, so we scheduled a meeting.

The next week, Latisha showed up at my office with a neatly organized binder that contained her budget, a printout of a spreadsheet that showed her income, details about all of her debt, and pertinent tax information. My immediate thought was, *Most people with "hopeless financial situations" don't show up with such organized files.* I rolled up my sleeves and went to work.

As I reviewed Latisha's income and budget, I learned that although she was earning a very good income, she was living paycheck to paycheck, so I dug in to see what was going on. What I discovered was that paying her debt was consuming _all_ her disposable income. At that time, Latisha had some pretty hefty student loans, a small amount of credit card debt, a car payment, a personal loan she had taken out to fund her move to the area a few years earlier, and a debt consolidation loan she had taken out with her credit union. While functioning on such a tight budget, Latisha had accumulated very little in savings and had almost nothing set aside in an emergency fund. Consequently, every time there was a bump in the road, she was forced to use her credit cards, which slowly put her further into debt. Her only consistent savings was her contribution of 3 percent in her 401(k), the minimum required to receive the maximum matching funds from her employer.

I immediately began analyzing Latisha's income and expenses and found that she was living a pretty lean existence. There was only one place I could find where she could cut a little. She was spending about thirty dollars a week eating lunch out, and she was willing to give that up to improve her finances. That freed up about $120 per month. One other thing stood out during my review was that Latisha was paying more than 12 percent interest on her personal loan, and it was costing her about five hundred dollars a month! I asked Latisha about her credit and found out it was not great, but it was decent. I also asked about the credit union loan and found that she had paid back about half of the principal and had always paid it on time. Half of the credit union principal would be almost exactly enough to pay off the high-interest personal loan. I suggested that Latisha visit her credit union and ask if they would refinance the loan. My thought was *Because she had paid as agreed, they would probably be willing to loan her the original amount.* She could use it to pay off the personal loan, freeing up six hundred dollars a month.

She left my office saying she would pursue my suggestion. I was hopeful yet hesitant to get too excited, because I had heard the same thing from other people many times before. What I learned was that Latisha was a woman of action! At around 1:00 the very next afternoon, I was sitting at my desk when the phone rang; it was Latisha. Her voice, which was usually calm and quiet, sounded giddy and excited. She told me she was at the credit union, and things looked good. She had explained her situation to the credit union representative, and he was pretty sure they could make the loan refinance happen. She said in a tone that sounded both surprised and relieved, "I think this is going to work!" I couldn't have been happier for her. Over the next several days, the credit union finalized Latisha's refinance loan, and Latisha called me with an update. She had gotten a slightly lower interest rate, which lowered the credit union payment by about forty dollars a month. The credit union took care of paying off the high-interest personal loan, creating a savings of five hundred a month. This gave her some immediate breathing room and much-needed peace of mind. Combined with the lunch savings, Latisha had gone from living paycheck to paycheck to having a $660 budget surplus in a matter of a few days!

Latisha was thrilled with her cash flow improvement and was ready for the next step! We met again to continue the conversation and decide on the most advantageous use for the "found" $660. When you think about it, it's pretty amazing that in less than a week, Latisha had created all of these monthly savings with very little impact on her lifestyle.

Pack Lunch ($30/week)	$120
Refinance Credit Union Loan	$40
Pay Off Personal Loan	$500
	$660

During our second meeting, Latisha revealed her primary financial goals were to pay off debt, fund her retirement, build her emergency fund, and have enough disposable income to travel and enjoy life. The gaping hole I saw in Latisha's financial picture was what would happen to her financially if she became seriously ill and was unable to work for a significant period of time. She was single, so her entire income depended on her ability to work. Although she had long-term disability insurance at work, that would provide only about 60 percent of her income, and she needed 100 percent. I suggested a life insurance policy with living benefits. She was young and healthy, so the cost was less than $50 a month, which was a small price to pay for the protection and peace of mind it provided. In addition to the death benefit that all life insurance provides, the policy gave her access to up to 90 percent of the death benefit in the event she became terminally, critically, or chronically ill. That way, she could continue funding her life without depleting her emergency and retirement savings. Her living benefits policy would provide a check written to Latisha that she could use to pay whatever expenses she needed. It could pay her mortgage or medical bills, put food on the table, or allow her to access care and treatment that her medical insurance might not cover. More than anything else, it gave her the comfort of knowing she was protected if a catastrophic illness or injury occurred.

As I said, Latisha was (and still is) truly a woman of action. Once she got the much-needed breathing room, she became a woman on a mission to continue improving her financial situation. She budgeted $150 a month to build her emergency fund, and she used the remaining surplus to aggressively pay down her remaining credit card debt. Within a year, she had paid off half of her credit card debt and was on track to pay off her car in a few months. Once the car was paid off, she attacked the credit card debt with even more determination, and within six months she had completely paid that off too. Latisha went from barely scraping by and living paycheck to paycheck to having a monthly budget surplus of over one thousand dollars and protection against becoming seriously ill. This was when things got really fun for Latisha.

With only her student loans and the credit union loan left, both with reasonable interest rates, Latisha was ready to ramp up her retirement savings. I helped her open a tax-free retirement account, and she began contributing five hundred dollars a month. She is currently on track to fully fund her retirement by age sixty-five, be debt free and well protected.

Many women, even when they believe their financial situation is hopeless, find that they are doing most things right. Latisha learned that there is no such thing as a hopeless financial situation. As long as you are willing to change the things that are not working for you, every situation has hope and a solution.

She also learned that a small tweak can often turn everything around. If you find yourself in a situation that feels hopeless, allow someone else to take a peek with a fresh set of eyes. It could create a miraculous turnaround for you too, just like it did for Latisha. Finally, always remember that knowing what to do is not enough—you must take action. Be a woman of action.

ERICA
MOORE

"Hosting Wine, Women and Wealth is one of the things I really enjoy about my work with Five Rings Financial! My background in computer sciences also makes me super analytical, so I also really love the numbers and problem-solving aspect of working individually with clients. Most of all, I'm proud that I help people find the fastest, safest and easiest path from where they are to where they want to be financially."

A Little about Erica

Erica Moore is a Regional Vice President with Five Rings Financial, where she has worked since 2011. She loves finance and numbers and has always had a passion for helping people. Erica first became involved in the financial industry more than twenty years ago because she wanted to make a positive impact on the financial lives of the people in her community. Since that time, she has realized she can't do it alone. Aligning with Five Rings Financial has allowed her to hire, mentor and train other agents in order to serve more people.

come to market her new business, but what happened for her when she attended was so much more than that.

Brooke's story, written a year after her first event.

> I was very new to networking when I found Wine, Women and Wealth. I was trying to learn how to be a network marketer and trying to find other female business owners who were also trying to "own their lives", grow businesses, and find balance. At the first meeting I went to, I felt like I had found a safe place to grow, laugh, love, and learn. The connections I've made have become lifelong friendships. I have learned to grow as a person and ask for help with challenges. I found a place to ask for resources, have been inspired to open new lines of communication with my spouse, and opened my mind to ideas and strategies about money. I hadn't realized I was so closed off about money! My relationships have become stronger. My financial picture has more promise, and overall, I am happier. I am very thankful for this group and look forward to it every month.

While Brooke came with the expectation of networking for her business, she became even more excited when she learned about the financial empowerment and education we provide. She especially saw the importance and need of living benefits, a tool that provides funds to help pay for medical bills, the house payment, the car payment, and even food on the table should one become sick with a terminal, critical, or chronic illness. Brooke loved the idea of protecting her family and assets with living benefits.

Did I mention that Brooke was the primary breadwinner in her household? That being said, without her income and that of her husband, her family would be in deep trouble. She was hungry for information to make her financial household stronger. Although it wasn't always easy between her corporate job, her wellness business, and her family, Brooke found the time to attend some of our other educational classes and learn how to protect the money she had already saved, along with saving even more money each month. She joined us at Wine, Women and Wealth every month and attended Money 101 a couple of times as well.

After doing her due diligence and getting comfortable with these new concepts, Brooke put all of the pieces in place to provide living benefits for her husband and herself. Because her husband's career required him to travels constantly, this brought her great peace of mind. She knew her family would not be financially damaged if she got sick (or worse) because she had protected her own income with that living benefits policy.

Fast forward to the future, about a year after her first Wine, Women and Wealth. With the friendships she developed at the events she attended, Brooke was able to come to the realization that she still had to "keep her day job" and look at her network marketing business as more of a "passion project". It's fun seeing her team up with other wellness people in our WW&W community. I've seen her confidence grow so much as she became smarter about networking and making deeper connections. She so enjoys the topics we cover at our events that she began reading more books on those concepts! Best of all, she was finally able to take control and stand in her own power about her finances.

DALEY KROM

*"As a hostess of Wine, Women and Wealth,
I love having the opportunity to meet new and
amazing women each month. I never know who
is going to walk through the door and share her
amazing story with us!*

*"I enjoy educating people about how money
works, but my true passion is helping women feel
empowered when it comes to money decisions. Wine,
Women and Wealth is a safe, warm environment for
women to come into and ask scary questions without
feeling judged or belittled. It's a place to learn
something new, as well as a place to just get out and
be in the company of girlfriends. It's a place for all
women to come and just "be"... to show up as their
authentic selves. Every month, my life is changed by
great women like Brooke, who not only became my
client, she also became one of my best friends."*

A Little about Daley

Daley has the unique perspective of being the daughter of the co-founders of Five Rings Financial, so you might expect that she has always worked in the family business and always had a love for numbers and money. Not so! It wasn't until 2014, after some life-changing challenges, that she took a hard look at the business she'd been around all of her life and decided to become an agent. As she helped clients learn about money, she began feeling comfortable and empowered when it came to her own skills and education. Daley feels passionate about educating all Americans on how money works and empowering people to believe in themselves while helping them make sound financial choices. In fact, she's so passionate that she rose to the rank of Executive Vice President within seventeen months of beginning her Five Rings career.

Daley lives in northern Colorado with her husband and is mother to two handsome boys. Her vision and purpose in this life is to heal financial strife and empower others so that we can all live as our most abundant and financially worthy selves.

Camilla (and Laura)
Finding Community in Unfamiliar Territory

by Elizabeth Hansen

I moved to Billings, Montana, in the spring of 2015. Not long thereafter, I began my career with Five Rings Financial. I started building our Wine, Women and Wealth community from scratch and began to attract the most phenomenal women in Montana. Having just moved to a new state and not knowing a ton of people myself, I posted invitations to our events on social media platforms, such as Meetup and Facebook. Unbeknownst to me, there were two other women who were new to Billings and were using social media to meet new people as well. Luckily, Camilla and Laura happened upon Wine, Women and Wealth and decided to come.

Camilla had recently moved to Billings from Florida to be closer to her daughter and grandchildren. Although she did have her family close by, she really didn't know anyone else. Camilla had been a successful interior designer for many years and truly enjoyed helping others create beautiful homes interiors that they loved and deserved. Unfortunately, when she moved, she took a job that she ended up despising. The environment was stressful, including office politics and micromanagement. Camilla also had recently been through a terrible divorce, which shook her self-confidence to the core and left her feeling anxious about her future in every way, especially because the divorce had left her bank account quite empty. According to Stephen Jenkins, a professor at the London School of Economics, "Despite the common perception that women make out better than men in divorce proceedings, women who worked before, during, or after their marriages see a 20 percent decline in income when their marriages end". Camilla was definitely feeling that blow. She found Wine, Women and Wealth on Meetup and decided to come, try to learn something new about money, and maybe meet some new people. At the end of the evening, we got a chance to talk more and decided to meet for coffee the following day.

When I sat down with Camilla, to say she was a broken version of her formerly glorious self would be an understatement. She hated her job but was afraid to leave because of her financial situation. She was worried about paying for the upcoming holidays and wondered how she was ever going to get ahead financially. Worst of all, she felt alone. She had devoted herself to her job and family but hadn't had a chance to create the community of friends that she had left behind in Florida. Her loneliness was compounded because she didn't want to burden her daughter with her fears and concerns. How wonderful would it be to have a friend, a confidant whom she could share with, and even more important someone with whom to socialize and have fun!

Laura had also recently moved to Billings following the death of her husband. She began substitute teaching in the local elementary school district and enjoyed her time, but she had not yet made any deep connections in the area. Something was missing: she was also looking for a soul sister in whom she could confide. At the advice of her daughter, Laura began searching out new ways to connect via Facebook. Laura has a beautiful, caring, giving spirit, and she had a great vision for starting a scholarship fund. She wanted to discuss how we could help get her set up and who else in the community would be interested in joining her. We also decided to have coffee following Wine,

Women and Wealth, and at that meeting I suggested that she should speak with Camilla. Camilla and Laura had been at the same Wine, Women and Wealth event the night before, but they had not connected with each other. After sharing their contact information, they decided to get together for their own coffee date. It was friendship at first sight! Ever since that day, the two have been virtually inseparable, and it couldn't have come at a better time.

Not long after Camilla and Laura's friendship began, Camilla received another devastating blow: she had received an offer to start with a new national design company! She jumped at the chance to leave the job she despised so much. She gave her two weeks' notice and began setting up her in-home office. However, not two days after she started her new job, she was "let go" and found out that the only reason she had been hired was so the new design firm could pirate all of her clients and contractors! Now without a job and already stressed out about money, Camilla's anxiety went into overdrive. It was no surprise that she came down with a severe case of bronchitis. During that week, Laura stopped by to check on her new friend with books and home-made chicken soup. Camilla was still recovering when I stopped in to visit her about a week later, and I was surprised to see that she was beside herself with excitement. While she was sick and stuck at home, and with no job to go back to, she had begun learning all about LinkedIn, a social media platform that helps professionals make business connections. She had started building a huge community of people all over the world! However, she had no idea what to do with all of her newfound knowledge and ways of reaching so many more people.

As much as I wished I could have helped her save for retirement or set up an account with living benefits, I knew she would have to wait until she was a little more financially stable. However,

I was determined to help her in whatever way I could. I encouraged her to take her new knowledge, along with her many years of experience in interior design and put it all together by marketing herself on LinkedIn. She began blogging and sharing great design tips on social media. She increased her exposure and contact base around the world. In fact, many people began seeking her out as a consultant to help them get the same great results she was getting on LinkedIn. Starting one's own business can be nerve-wracking, exhilarating, scary, and fun all at once. Fortunately, Camilla has an entrepreneurial spirit and the gumption to make this business her own. She also has the love, support, and encouragement of Laura and her new community of friends from Wine, Women and Wealth.

One of the best features of WW&W is the formal networking portion that we do at each event. We get to learn about all of the women in the room and what their passions are. It's a great way for attendees to market themselves, and I was sure that once Camilla shared her beautiful design portfolio, there would be lots of women in our community who would love to use her services. I realized this was how I could help Camilla! This was how she could help herself get her new business off the ground!

Camilla loved and truly believed in the financial products that we offer, as well as our approach to retirement and college savings. And while being an agent with us wasn't necessarily what she wanted to do with the rest of her career, she was able to plug into our system by becoming a referral agent. She could earn extra income while she builds the business she's passionate about by simply referring her friends to our events.

These days, Camilla comes to every Wine, Women and Wealth she can! She enthusiastically markets her business, and with each event, I see her confidence grow—and her business grow as well! And Camilla doesn't come alone. She and Laura come together, and they always share how they became best friends and built their own community of girlfriends through Wine, Women and Wealth.

ELIZABETH HANSEN

"Five Rings Financial is a different kind of financial services company that has a collaborative, family-based culture. Even our mission statement reflects our heart-based approach. For me, the best part is the last paragraph – "It is the dream of a place where the hurting, the frustrated, the disillusioned and the confused can find love, acceptance, help, hope, guidance and encouragement. It is a home for people that need a second chance or a third chance or however many chances it takes."

This 'heart' filters into all aspects of Five Rings, from our Money 101 and Wine, Women and Wealth programs to how we work one-on-one with our clients, to how we hire new agents. Camilla's story is a great example of how heart is the common thread of all things Five Rings."

A Little about Elizabeth

With a doctorate in physical therapy, Elizabeth Hansen has always loved helping people. After graduating, Elizabeth embraced her new medical career wholeheartedly, working long hours as a clinic director. However, seven years later, when she and her husband decided to start a family, Elizabeth had to decide how to merge a career with motherhood. Her goal was to work part-time to stay home a little more while her children were babies, with an eye to move back into clinical work when they went to school. Originally, she sought out part-time opportunities in physical therapy but found she would be overqualified and underpaid for most of those.

Elizabeth spoke with her good friend Daley Krom (also a collaborator of this book) about becoming an agent with Five Rings Financial. Elizabeth thought that this might be the perfect way to work around her husband's schedule and spend more time with her two girls. She already knew a lot about the company because her parents, like Daley's, had been agents with Five Rings for many years. Since then, Elizabeth opened the first Five Rings Financial Agency in Montana and has found the perfect career fit of helping people with their finances and balancing motherhood. She is so excited about this that she has developed a new Five Rings program, called Money, Mommy and Me, for parents to help their children become financially educated.

Cornelia
"You Just Don't Know What's Around the Corner"

by Nicole Aspenson

In 2011, I began researching what it would take to begin a career in financial services. Initially, I was really disappointed with what was "out there". Fortunately, through Wine, Women and Wealth, I found Five Rings Financial. I am so delighted to be partnered with such a high-integrity organization to pursue my passion educating and empowering people, especially women, to find financial freedom on their own terms.

You see, one of the women I was able to help was invited to Wine, Women and Wealth by a mutual friend in 2013. Cornelia had been attending Wine, Women and Wealth for about three years, working on her money mind-set and trying to figure out a new career path that she could be passionate enough about to leave her corporate job. She discovered that passion and enrolled in a training course to help her pursue a new career as a speaker, coach, and corporate trainer.

I always do a little drawing for a prize when I host a Wine, Women and Wealth event. In 2016, Cornelia won the raffle! The prize was a book about tax-free index accounts, one of our most powerful tools for building retirement plans. She got excited about saving for her future in a safe financial vehicle, where she could get the upside of the market without the risk of losing any money due to market performance. She was even more excited when she learned about the power of living benefits. Then she asked me whether this could work for college savings for her eight-year-old daughter. My response was, "Why, yes! That's one of our specialties. We call it our Million-Dollar Baby Plan!" We met the very next week to discuss things further.

Here's Cornelia's summary of the meeting.

> I met Nicole about five years ago at a Wine, Women and Wealth event. I liked the message of the event, Nicole's knowledge about the products, and her caring heart for everyone she meets.

> Over the next couple of years, we built a relationship, and I learned more about investment ideas, especially the life insurance with living benefits and tax-free retirement options. I went to Money 101 and read the book *The Retirement Miracle*, by Patrick Kelly and I gained an even better understanding of what I could do. I decided living benefits was a great idea. I went through the requirements, such as a health check, and came out as the top 2 percent rating for health.

Cornelia loved the tax-free index account and wanted to get one started for herself in the future when her new business was more financially stable, because she was in transition from her corporate job to her new career as a trainer, speaker, and coach.
Of course, as moms do, Cornelia put her daughter first and started a college savings plan for her eight-year-old. While we were discussing the tax-free college savings (aka our Million Dollar Baby Plan), Cornelia initially thought that she personally didn't need a life insurance policy. She explained that her daughter's father was a good dad and would take care of their daughter if Cornelia died too soon. I then asked the hard question. "What

about *you*? What would happen if you couldn't go to work for six months? Or a year? How would you pay your mortgage and utilities, or keep food on the table for you and your daughter?" We discussed how she could access a big pile of cash should she suffer a chronic, critical or terminal illness, like a heart attack, stroke, or cancer. It only took a minute, and she said, "Wow, how could somebody *not* do that? It just makes sense!" With that, we put Cornelia's living benefits plan in place on the spot.

About eighteen months later, I got a call from Cornelia. We'd seen each other at Wine, Women and Wealth events, but this time she had something important to tell me and wanted to do so privately. She explained that during her last checkup and colonoscopy, her doctor had discovered she had cancer.

Cornelia's own words.

> In March 2016, I was diagnosed with colon cancer. I had to undergo surgery, and they found a metastatic tumor, which required chemotherapy treatment. During the therapy, I called Nicole because I wanted to get some money out of the insurance to pay for my out-of-pocket expenses, like copayments and optional treatments. Nicole informed me that I could access much more than I was hoping for, which was a very positive surprise! I was on medical leave and state disability, and although it was helpful, that money was not enough to pay for my needs. I also opted for comprehensive and sometimes alternative care, such as acupuncture, essential oils, herbs, and a very organic diet, which were not covered by my health insurance plan. With the money from my life insurance, I was able to fight my cancer on my own terms, and I did

not have to worry about going into debt by running up my credit cards.

Cornelia had been hoping I could help her access five thousand dollars to pay the deductible for her health insurance. She was so overwhelmed by the large deductible that she hadn't even imagined what other expenses were in her future. The insurance company was so helpful and easy to work with, and even though Cornelia had taken out her policy only about a year and a half earlier, her claim was approved and paid within two weeks. Even though Cornelia had paid in only about $1,300 in premiums on her life insurance policy, she could now access up to $325,000, in cash, tax free. She was in shock—in a good way, of course.

Cornelia shares.
> Having access to over $300,000 gave me options ...
> I didn't have to go back to my old job. I had the free-
> dom to do what I wanted. I also had no debt, which
> made life a lot more comfortable. It also gave me the
> freedom to pursue the career I am passionate about:
> speaking, training, and coaching.

It took Cornelia a couple days for the financial relief to sink in. We discussed that she could exercise the entire amount or take a portion now and have a year from her diagnosis to file an election for more. She initially opted to take 50 percent, and eight months later when we filed for the second election, she qualified for terminal illness and had a higher percentage available. She also opted to leave fifty thousand dollars of life insurance in place for future needs.

Right after her diagnosis, Cornelia had contacted a cancer treatment center in New Hampshire. She had done her research and felt that this was her very best option for recovery. When they told her the cost, much of which was not covered by insurance, she sadly had to tell them that she could not afford it. Once I handed her the benefit check, Cornelia was able to check in at the alternative treatment center without worrying about the expense.

Not only was she able to use the funds to recover, but she was also able to visit her family in Germany, whom she hadn't seen in three years. When her father passed away two months after her visit, she was so grateful to have spent that time with him while he was still alive. She also took her daughter to Hawaii, was able to access other alternative treatments, and could focus on healing rather than having to worry about finances. You see, living benefits covers more than just medical expenses; they provide money to allow you to keep living your life.

Cornelia sums it all up.

> I do not know if the cancer will return at some point, so I have also invested in another product with Nicole that gives me the upside potential of the market without any downside risk. That gives me peace of mind! I would highly recommend everybody have living benefits insurance. If nothing happens to your health, then there will be a nice sum of money to draw from in later years.
>
> Getting living benefits was one of my better decisions ... So, if somebody is considering getting living benefits, I would remind you to listen to my story and absolutely get the living benefits, because you just don't know what's around the corner.

I never imagined that Cornelia would need to activate the living benefits. I felt blessed to have such remarkable tools to offer before this experience, and since seeing how much they helped Cornelia battle her cancer, I have become even more passionate about telling everyone about living benefits!

***

To see Cornelia's testimonial video, go to the Wine, Women and Wealth website: https://www.winewomenwealth.org

NICOLE ASPENSON

"I am so grateful that I was able to be the one to provide Cornelia with a financial safety net when she needed it most. Preparing for your financial future is one of the most important steps you can take in life. The mission of Five Rings Financial is to empower and educate everyone, especially women. That mission, the heartfelt leadership of my mentors, and the Wine, Women and Wealth events I host allow me to provide this same safety net for so many others."

A Little about Nicole

Nicole J. Aspenson is making finances fun! Her compassionate, genuine and warm-hearted nature is what her clients love most about her.

After watching her mother lose half of her 401(k) only two years before she'd planned on retiring, Nicole began researching a career in financial services. She was initially disappointed with the professional options she found. With a desire to help her mom and others like her retire with dignity, she continued to search.

Fortunately, through persistence, Nicole found Five Rings

Financial. Now, Nicole is able to pursue her passion. From finding strategies for creating an income that can't be outlived to building financial legacies, she provides solutions for managing risk and preparing for even those unforeseen obstacles that may lie ahead. She works with each individual, family and business in a one-on-one environment to develop personalized strategies given your particular situation.

Nicole is a sought-after speaker, a financial coach, and an expert at connecting people and gathering resources for her clients. An Executive Vice President with Five Rings Financial and founder of Anchor Financial Agency -- a division of Five Rings Financial, Nicole works diligently to gently guide her clients through the learning process to anchor their financial future!

Sandra and Lydia
"My Husband Does That. And He Did, Until …"

by Monica Wilk

By the time 2012 rolled around, I had been in the financial services world for almost twenty years. However, I had invested this time on the corporate side with one of the world's largest financial companies as a medical life underwriter, assisting agents and marketing companies to place their business with consumers. As I grew in my career specialty and realized the significance of just how important financial education can be to families, I had a desire to find a way to break out of the "corporate-underwriter-employee" role and work with clients directly on the marketing side. Not only did I understand, firsthand the important role that financial products can play in a person's most challenging times, but I also had a special passion to assist women who were single or divorced and experiencing the same types of issues that I had gone through personally. Unfortunately, in my two decades of experience, almost all of my exposure to the marketing side of the industry was with men and male-dominated agencies. Seemingly, it was over 90 percent men selling to men, with not a women's program in sight! Then Five Rings Financial and Wine, Women and Wealth divinely appeared on my life path. Through my five years of experience with Five Rings, I believe these stories, which are very similar, truly illustrate just how powerful this women's financial literacy program is and how critically important it became for these two women.

Sandra

First, let me introduce Sandra. Sandra came as a guest to our Wine, Women and Wealth event about six months after our initial meeting in Cedar Rapids, Iowa. Our WW&W community had been growing steadily with a group of fantastic women who consisted of family members, close friends, and a few "power partners" who each valued our mission of empowering women in the community with our financial education platform. As is the case in each of our events, each guest and regular attendee is encouraged to introduce herself and share any story she wishes about herself, her financial background, or her experiences.

Whenever Sandra introduced herself, she repeated a story that we hear over and over each time we hold an event. She'd say, "I love and appreciate all that you are doing for women and their finances, and I'm having a wonderful time with all of you, but my husband takes care of all of our finances and has done so for our entire thirty-plus years of marriage. He is really good at it, and I have always felt very secure in his decisions and in his handling of our affairs." Sandra became a regular at our meetings and fell in love with the companionship and the new friends she was making. She regularly invited friends of her own and became quite an advocate for the way we teach financial principals in a fun and exciting environment. But each time we got around to the introductions, Sandra would repeat, "My husband takes care of all of this, and he does a great job." And he did, until ...

I can remember the day so vividly when Sandra called and said her husband had died unexpectedly in a car accident. Although seemingly in good health, her husband had suffered a massive heart attack during an accident and died instantly on the side of the road. Obviously, Sandra went through the all-too-familiar experience of being left alone and in shock from the sudden death of her spouse. As challenging a situation that this could be for anyone, imagine the increased hardship if her financial affairs had not been in order! Luckily for Sandra, her husband really had done a great job and left her with some life insurance and a few accounts that would help her get her feet back on the ground. Unfortunately, the representative whom Sandra's husband had worked with for years seemed very uninterested in assisting her through this transition; in fact, he even refused to return her calls.

That was when Sandra remembered her friends at Wine, Women and Wealth and called for help. Through a series of consultations and appointments, Sandra chose to place a portion of her money in a program that would continue to grow at reasonable interest rates but potentially eliminate any future losses. She had learned a lot about money and financial planning through her years of experience with WW&W, and she knew she had choices! She preferred the conservative approach of watching her money grow with guaranteed interest rates and low maintenance, knowing that she would have income for life that allowed her to enjoy her family and travel in retirement. Sandra was so happy about her decision and our program that she included a note in her annual Christmas letter to all her friends and relatives telling everyone how much she appreciated her friend Susie and all the women of WW&W who gave her the strength and security to get through the most difficult time in her life.

Lydia

Lydia was one of the original guests at our Cedar Rapids Wine, Women and Wealth. She has been a personal friend of my mother's for almost forty years, and she and her husband were like second parents to me. Lydia was one of my greatest supporters from day one, and she still is! She and her husband, Larry, were business owners and had pretty much counted on their business to be their retirement program. Much like Sandra's story, each time Lydia introduced herself, she would say, "My husband takes care of all the finances, and he's really good at it." And he did, and he was, until …

Just a year or so after Lydia began attending WW&W, she and Larry sold their business and planned on using all of the money from the sale of their business for their secure retirement.

They were so excited as they began to make their plans for retirement. As business owners, it was always hard to find time for vacations and travel. Now, they could finally visit all the places on their bucket list! Then out of nowhere, Larry started to have severe back pains. Through a series of tests, one of the worst-case scenarios came back: cancer. Suddenly all of their dreams went out the window.

In less than a year, Larry passed away, and now Lydia had to step in and take over the finances—something she had not been involved with previously. In the year before her husband passed away, their retirement savings had lost almost 20 percent of its value. Not only due to a declining market but also from the fees that were charged on the account. As Lydia said, "I was paying more in fees than my account was making each year! The representative who was handling my account had me 100 percent at risk in the stock market, and I was seventy-one years old. Even though I wasn't a financial planner, I knew that couldn't be right!" Once again, the many months of attendance at Wine, Women and Wealth helped Lydia understand that she had alternatives. She contacted us, and we were able to place her money in a secure, reasonable interest rate environment that had the potential to never lose money and guarantee her an income for life. She calls it "Sleep Insurance" because she never has to worry about money for the rest of her life.

I wish these were the only two women who attend our Wine, Women and Wealth workshops and state that their husbands "take care of all that," but they're not. Unfortunately, it seems to be echoed among quite a few of our guests. It's not that we encourage women to take over the finances; we simply want them to be great financial partners to their spouses, have a true understanding of their financial picture, and know what's going on. Our hope is that by continuing to spread the word through this social-educational format, we can help couples in making sure that everyone is involved in the process of achieving financial independence and security.

There are many wonderful ways that Wine, Women and Wealth has changed the lives of so many women, including mine! I feel truly blessed.

MONICA WILK

"One of the best things about Sandra's story is that one of our guests, Susie Makinster, fell in love with our mission of Wine, Women and Wealth from day one. She felt so great about it that she decided to become a referral agent with Five Rings Financial. Susie was actually a close friend of Sandra's and had originally invited her to our event. Imagine the pride she feels in knowing that although a serious tragedy happened to her good friend, she was able to help Sandra overcome her fears about money and set her on a course for peace of mind and security.

"It's so exciting to be in the financial education industry, especially with the Five Rings Family. We are so different from the typical financial agency. We believe that men and women, are equally important to the future of our industry, and we offer an equal opportunity to all employees to have amazing careers. We believe that educating all Americans on the principles of how money works is crucial. This is truly valuable information that can save the future of families and impact generations to come!"

A Little about Monica

Monica comes to us from Cedar Rapids, Iowa, with more than twenty-five years of experience in the financial industry. She has a fifteen-year corporate financial background in underwriting at Transamerica Life Insurance. In 2007, following her desire to work as an agent helping individuals, couples, and families, Monica transitioned to a marketing and agent role with her parent company. In 2013, she found her true calling when she joined Five Rings Financial.

Monica's passion for helping people is heightened through Five Rings' Wine, Women and Wealth, bringing awareness, education, and inspiration to women to propel them on a path of financial independence. Monica loves being with, working with, and supporting her husband, Mike (Five Rings founder and CEO) as they travel around the United States meeting new people, spreading the word on how money works, and changing people's lives.

Lilly
Promises Kept

by Mary Glynn Fisher

Before I met Five Rings Financial, which was not long after the birth of our son, I was ready to reenter the business world. To accelerate the process, I initiated and hosted a networking and empowerment lunch in my community. This group attracted wonderful, professional men and women. Great people brought great people. It was an event I always looked forward to, which was important because it took a lot of motivation for me to leave my cute baby boy! It's funny how one thing leads to another. I had no idea how hosting this networking event and meeting the people I met there would reshape my destiny. It was through this event that I met Heather Brinkman, and we immediately knew we would be friends for a long time. I loved her engaging personality and fantastic work ethic.

Not long after I met Heather, we were introduced to Mike Wilk, the founder and CEO of Five Rings Financial. That meeting was a turning point for both of us. We caught the vision of sharing the basics and fundamentals of a personal financial education with hundreds of thousands of Americans and then helping them to apply what they have learned to reach their financial aspirations. We were so inspired that we decided to join this company together. To this day, Heather continues to be one of my closest friends and most successful partners.

Five Rings Financial operates much like a real estate brokerage, with sub-agencies across the country that are branded, supported, and overseen by our home office in Littleton, Colorado. Heather and I were so excited to be launching the first Five Rings agency in Virginia! Mike encouraged us to incorporate Denise Arand's Wine, Women and Wealth concept in our business plan, so when Heather was visiting the San Diego area, she decided to attend one of the events Denise was hosting there. Heather was excited by what she saw, and before she boarded the plane to fly home to Virginia, she called and said, "Mary, we can do this!" And we have, impacting thousands of lives along the way. My friend Lilly is one of them.

One day, my bubbly friend Janet brought Lilly, her colleague from the fashion industry, to our networking lunch. Lilly made a great impression and was professional, warm, beautiful, well-dressed, and well-spoken. We learned that not only was she was a fashion consultant, but this talented lady was also a working actor and producer as well as a philanthropist.

Over time, we began a great friendship, sharing a love for personal growth and helping people. A visit with Lilly was always time well spent. She's one of the most fair, generous, and inspiring people I know.

Lilly and I had been friends for about four years when I began working at Five Rings Financial. She was so supportive and interested in everything Five Rings! Lilly came to Money 101, our monthly educational dinner. She also came to Wine, Women and Wealth as often as possible and brought a friend or two with her every time.

After a while, Lilly asked if I would be willing to help her parents with some of her accounts. It was my pleasure to do so. Her mother and father, born in the Philippines, were very hard working and loving. They both had served in the US Navy as nurses. I felt privileged to help such fantastic people protect and grow the retirement funds they had worked so hard for all of their lives.

Sometime after that, Lilly asked me if I could, as she put it, "Look at her financial stuff." I was honored to be invited.

From Lilly.

I do not believe in coincidences. The relationship I have developed with Mary and Five Rings has evolved and significantly impacted my life. Not only has it been amazing for me to be around people of such passion and purpose, but I feel a great sense of peace knowing that my money is protected! These connections have made a difference in all areas of my life.

To look back a few years, after Mary and her team helped my parents with some pressing needs, I invited her to have a look at my portfolio. I trusted her at that point and was open to learning how I might improve what had been a pretty good financial plan.

Mary introduced me to the CEO of Five Rings Financial, Mike Wilk, and I was impressed by this inspired and great man and everything he taught. Then I attended Money 101 and Wine, Women and Wealth many times. Each event reinforced what I heard about living benefits, safety and guarantees, and even great tax advantages. Those events also showed me how very different and special these people at Five Rings Financial are.

At some point, I asked Mary to meet with me. I invited her to my home, and we visited at my kitchen table. She made it clear that she was there to be helpful, not to sell me anything. She asked me about my goals, objectives, and dreams. And she listened. That was refreshing. She asked about my son, my family, my career, and my divorce. She truly wanted to understand how the tools she had at her disposal could benefit me. I am an extremely independent person. I had a good plan with a trusted wealth manager, but I was open to considering new possibilities.

I shared with her great things about my family, including my amazing siblings and their families. We talked about my son, my commitment to him, my love for him, and—gulp—how quickly the time would pass that would lead him to college and beyond.

I shared with her the challenges I had faced as well. How dramatically my life changed when my job in the corporate world—a job I loved with people I adored—disappeared almost overnight as our company of thousands was purchased and shut down. Then the divorce and how dedicated I was to navigate a good co-parenting relationship with my ex. Then buying my own home and managing my own portfolio. There were so many decisions that I had not expected to face in my mid-forties! I shared my philosophy on giving back to the community, my nonprofit work, and my entrepreneurial pursuits. Mary seemed to absorb every word while acknowledging how powerfully it seemed I had survived the difficulties.

She reviewed with me some of my options and how they might work for me, the advantages and disadvantages. There was no sales pressure, just fitting the possible puzzle pieces together. We left one another with "homework" to do and scheduled a date to visit again.

I am a strong and positive person nearly all the time, and when Mary left, I felt even more hopeful about my future.

Over the course of a few more visits, we were able to move a fair amount of my retirement savings into an account designed grow and protect my retirement with the option to turn into a stream of income (like a pension) when I reached retirement age. The money would only gain and would never lose principal or interest. It would protect my savings from market volatility and loss. We also created a "tax-free retirement" account, leveraging little-known tax advantages that can be achieved using a properly designed life insurance policy as a savings vehicle. We put living benefits life insurance in place; not only would this provide my son a tax-free, hassle-free cash payout when I pass away, BUT it could provide me with a large sum of cash to spend as I chose should I experience a catastrophic illness or accident. This created a safety net for me and my retirement savings.

As a disciplined, healthy person, regular exerciser, and yoga practitioner, I certainly didn't anticipate becoming ill. However, I realized it made sense to have these great options. My advice to everyone is if you understand the importance of life insurance, and if you can get it, it makes sense to have the kind with living benefits.

I was compelled to invite everyone to hear this important information. It became very natural for me to invite the people I cared most about—my family, my friends, and those in my communities—to these great events and to encourage them to talk to Mary about improving their plans, like I had improved mine. I knew what she had to offer would help reach their financial goals! Mary sat me down and explained the benefits of becoming a licensed referral agent. I took a class, studied, and passed my exam. Sometime later, I received my first commission check... it was a nice-sized check! Mary and I both had lumps in our throats and tears in our eyes. "Promises kept." We help people, and we get paid—in that order.

As I write this all these years later, promises have been kept. My son is thriving in college. My mom is having some medical issues that require a lot of attention and energy right now, and I feel privileged to be able to help my parents as best as I can. I feel great peace of mind that my money is growing safely and that Mary and the team at Five Rings are keeping their promises to me and to those whom I've introduced to them. This gives me great confidence as I move into this next phase of life.

I love the integrity. I love the passion for changing lives. Thank you for the partnership, Mary, Mike, and all the folks at Five Rings. Keeping promises: that's what Five Rings Financial means to me.

People say that a man's self-esteem is tied to his money and income. Well, ask any woman, and it's likely true for her too! It's not about the amount but about the ability to have enough to care for oneself and one's family, as well as the freedom to fully experience life. If you get the money straight, that can make a huge difference in your life and legacy. That's why I am so grateful to have had the chance to help Lilly do exactly that.

MARY GLYNN FISHER

"Whatever glass ceiling life has put on your dreams, it's up to you to break through! We love helping people with that transformation every day at Five Rings Financial. And in turn, many of these fantastic people are compelled to do the same, at their own pace. We have an irresistible, inspiring, and reality-based message that translates across most every background, age, and culture! Together, we are flourishing at Five Rings."

A Little about Mary

Mary Glynn Fisher is a devoted mother, wife, sister, daughter, friend, and business partner. From Westfield, New Jersey, she has lived many places including the Washington, DC, area before making her home in Virginia Beach, Virginia, just after 9/11. She holds a BA from Marymount University and is a committed lifelong learner.

Fisher was introduced to Mike Wilk, president and founder of Five Rings Financial, in 2011 when she attended a Money 101 workshop at the invitation of a generous acquaintance. That "day of destiny" elevated her ability to comprehend how to give back and contribute in a powerful and significant way. Respectfully and powerfully incubating and mentoring career changers to serve their families and communities through Five Rings Financial is what Mary loves best!

She loves experiencing sunrises and sunsets, and she generally loves a beautiful view. She has a great love of music, reading (especially biographies), traveling, cruising, laughing, and enjoying time with her treasured family and friends.

My Own Story: A Lifelong Dream Arrives!

by Rita Boccuzzi

I sit here today, writing this chapter in awe and gratitude. I'm a woman, mother, wife, business owner, cancer survivor, and dreamer. My life's ups and downs have guided me on a path filled with learning, growth, and a knowing that I could create a fantastic and financially successful life. I simply had to figure out how!

The daughter of Italian immigrants and middle sister of two brothers, I grew up in Los Angeles in the '70s. My parents were friends with many other Italians, some abundantly wealthy and some just starting out. This juxtaposition created such curiosity in my little girl mind. I remember one of my dad's friends had the most beautiful mansion complete with marble, granite, and imported furniture from Italy. When his wealthy friends were at our house, my ears would perk up as they talked about their real estate investments, such as a shopping complex or an apartment building. These same friends talked about their travels back to the homeland and other luxuries.

I would listen to these conversations and wonder what made them different from my dad. My dad worked so diligently, so how come we didn't travel like they did? Why didn't we have the luxuries they did? How did they get the money for real estate investing? All of these questions flooded my mind and piqued my curiosity about money. How could I be like the wealthy Italians I knew? The more I listened, the more I dreamed of wealth and the luxuries it provided, like travels to the homeland. These dreams led me to start asking questions, which were met with statements like "It's not polite for young children to talk about these things" or "Young ladies aren't supposed to ask questions about private matters." I know they meant well, but how was I supposed to learn about money if I couldn't ask these questions?

As I got older, curiosity about money stuck with me and significantly influenced my young adult years. My older brother and I often talked about business and real estate investing. He bought his first investment property with his wife at the age of twenty-five. He was an entrepreneur and worked a traditional job while getting his new business off the ground. He was six years older than me and was my role model; I wanted to be just like him. Unexpectedly, he passed away in a tragic accident at the age of twenty-seven. I was in shock and heartbroken! Now who would I look up to? My brother was a source of positive influence and inspiration to me and so many others. While standing by his gravesite, I made a promise that I would continue his legacy of positive influence, inspiration, and love through my life.

My childhood financial curiosity and desire to leave a legacy motivated me to move forward with my dreams. The year after my brother passed away, I purchased my first property at the age of twenty-one. A year later, at twenty-two I married my wonderful husband, also an Italian immigrant. When life became hectic between wedding planning, dealing with my husband's immigration process, and trying to grieve and heal the loss of my brother, I dropped out of my last year of college, where I was studying to be a teacher. That lifelong dream seemed to disappear as my life was consumed with marriage, new motherhood, and work.

With everything my adult life brought, I began a career in the healthcare field. I was told it would be a stable field, and I hoped it would highlight my love of serving others. At first, it was a dream come true. I ended up with multiple promotions and a beautiful office, where I would often watch sunrises and sunsets. Time went on, and before I knew it, I'd been in healthcare for twenty years, and I had transitioned into the administrative and corporate side of the career. However, I had become more and more dissatisfied because I was pushing paper and missing my kids growing up. Late at night, I lay awake wondering what had happened to my life, my curiosity, my dreams, and my legacy. I decided it was time to honor the graveside promise that I'd made to myself and my big brother many years earlier.

With my desire reignited, I decided to follow in the footsteps of my brother and start an entrepreneurial venture on the side. I wanted to own my life! I had always tried to learn as much about money as possible but often found the door shut in my face by the financial industry because I didn't have six figures in my investment accounts. If I couldn't learn what to do, how would I ever grow that kind of money? My sons were getting older, and I wanted them to learn about money too. Voila! I would start a career in the financial industry; that way, I could learn what I wanted to and share it with my sons.

As a diligent student of my new career, I started studying at the library, reading books, and taking workshops on finances in my spare time. I committed to my own education and was determined to develop myself and learn everything I could about finance and how money worked. As I worked with different financial companies, I realized I had questions that still weren't getting answered. I was frustrated beyond belief. The financial services industry started to feel a lot like my corporate day job: frustration, confusion, and indifference. Plus, I found that I had to dress in pantsuits a lot because most of the "big box" financial companies had a dress code that essentially required women to dress like their male counterparts. It might not sound like a big deal, but I felt I was losing myself and who I was. It was disempowering to dress the part and have to act like a man, and it made me feel so out of integrity. I didn't realize finance was still so male-dominated—even today! My dream career had become a nightmare!

Ultimately, the stress at home, in my new career, and at my day job took a toll on me, and I got sick. I had inflamed tonsils and thought I had strep throat. I seriously didn't have time for this! I was a forty-three-year-old soccer mom who was busy with my family, my job, and the new career I was building. Things went from bad to worse when I found out that it wasn't strep—it was cancer.

With this cancer diagnosis, I felt an urgency to grab hold of life, find my dreams again, and create the life I had always dreamed of. Fighting cancer was expensive and definitely took a huge toll on my family's financial stability. Plus, I felt like a burden to my family. Thankfully, I went into remission, and from that point on, I renewed my commitment to get the financial education that I needed so I could be my own boss and teach my children how to be financially successful. I began studying wealth-building strategies with millionaires and billionaires who ran mentorship programs for money-curious people like me. I surrounded myself with successful people and learned from those who had figured it out. I didn't feel like I had time for mistakes. I ended up investing six figures in my financial self-education and leveraged what financial resources we had left to make this dream happen. I knew I had to change something in my life.

As I got stronger physically and financially, I felt inspired to create a financial literacy program. I had never seen finances taught the way I wanted to teach them. I didn't want to do this alone, so I prayed that there was someone out there with whom I could partner. I had a big vision and needed support. I knew there had to be someone out there wiser, smarter, and more experienced than me. I simply couldn't believe that I was the only one with the same vision to educate people on how money works. I worked diligently on my program and simultaneously kept myself open for a miracle.

Then my prayers were answered. An entrepreneur girlfriend of mine invited me to go to a woman's conference with her in Orange County. She was shy, and she wanted my "Italian energy" because, as the old saying goes, I've never met a stranger! I took this as a compliment, and because she was a dear friend who had always supported me, I cleared my schedule and we headed down to Orange County together. When it came time for the breakout sessions, we chose different topics. I felt guided to a session about women and finances.

The woman at front of the room, Mara, was this young, hip, vibrant gal with platinum hair and tattoos. She taught about the mind-set around money. I saw women in the room getting excited, laughing, and enjoying themselves as we talked about money. I felt like pinching myself! The lifelong dream I had always visualized was coming true. I knew divine intervention was at work. I was so excited that I ran up to meet the speaker, only for her to tell me that she was moving to Colorado that very night! The good news was she said she'd support me from

Colorado, and she invited me to check out a Wine, Women and Wealth event in Carlsbad, California.

A few weeks later, I attended my first Wine, Women and Wealth. I loved it! There were women laughing, learning, building community, collaborating, and feeling great about their money! Plus, no pantsuits! It was well worth the two-and-a-half-hour drive. It was life changing. This event was where I first met Denise Arand, the founder of Wine, Women and Wealth. I remember walking up to her at the end of the event and saying, "There are millions more women in Los Angeles. Why isn't this being done there? It's so desperately needed."

In her sweet, loving way, Denise looked me in the eye and simply replied, "Well, we were just waiting for you, darlin'."

Everything inside of me screamed, Yes! This is what I've been praying for my entire life! They were waiting for me, and I was waiting for them. They had the same mission and vision to educate women and middle-income Americans about how money works. They understood the big picture that if we help everyone, regardless of whether or not they have six-figure investment accounts, we could change the world. Women are the nurturers of society; if we help them, we help everyone. I truly believe if we raise up women, our economy will rise.

It was time to get to work. As I did my due diligence, I was given the opportunity to interview Mike Wilk, the CEO of this amazing company, on the phone. I must have asked at least fifty questions. Then I met with one of the founding partners, Lyall Donnelly, in person and asked him the same fifty questions to be sure they were in alignment. I was thrilled to find that they were! They invited me to check out their National Training Camp so I could see firsthand how they trained and taught their business associates and clients. Everything was in alignment with what I was looking for. It's amazing how fast things move when you finally know you're in the right place. I met Mara at the women's conference on October 30, 2014, and by January 20, 2015, I launched my first Wine, Women and Wealth in Burbank, California. My dream of being a teacher finally came full circle, however it came in a different package than I'd expected. And just like that, my dream of being a financial educator was launched, along with my budding new business.

Over the years, I've been working with Five Rings Financial and running Wine, Women and Wealth. These communities have grown across Los Angeles. I'm so blessed to have seen my lifelong vision and dream of authentic financial conversations and entrepreneurship come to fruition in a way that I never expected—and we are just getting started. Now I know I'll leave an incredible legacy!

Justin
So I
Grateful
& Blessed
we are Friends
Love you,
Rita

RITA
BOCCUZZI

"I love working with women who desire to take charge of their financial future, expand their knowledge, and build their confidence regarding money and wealth! Our Wine, Women and Wealth communities help women learn to feel great about money to transform how they think, plan, interact, and live out a successful financial life!"

A Little about Rita

Rita Boccuzzi is a financial intelligence expert. She is a coauthor of *Redefine Finance$ & Wealth—7 Insights to Dominate Your Economics* and *50 Empowering Wealth & Financial Mind-$hifts.* She is passionately committed to guiding women to achieve financial peace of mind, which includes transforming money conversations, releasing money confusion, expanding financial knowledge, and building confidence regarding money and wealth.

She is committed to teaching and learning through education processes. She has built wealth and lost it, and built it again, which has led her to study the development of wealth creation through successful programs.

Rita is a proven professional whose mission and commitment are to lead and inspire by educating and empowering women to achieve financial independence. She gets to the core of issues on how women relate to money and then teaches them practical strategies for managing that money.

She leads Wine, Women and Wealth events and Money 101 educational workshops in the Los Angeles area. She is CEO of Flourish Inc., a division of Five Rings Financial. She educates through her heartfelt mission to reform how people think, plan, interact, and live out their financial lives.

Tami
New Beginnings

by Kristen Judd

I first met Tami when I launched a new location for Wine, Women and Wealth in October 2015. She was quiet and took it all in. Little did I know at the time that she came for help, advice, and support. It was the first event in that town, and the women there were all getting to know each other. At most of our WW&W events, we spend some time talking about money personalities, tackling limiting beliefs about money, and even talking about practical ways to make and save more money. This event was no exception, and we had a great conversation about the "Romance of Finance" and the relationship women have with money.

Tami reached out to me the very next day and asked if I helped women who were going through a divorce. I told her I would love to see how I could support her. We set up an appointment and met the next week.

Tami found herself in that space that many women do at some point: You get married, start a life together, buy your first house, start having kids, and quit your career to stay home with them. Then one day, you find out the life you built with your spouse isn't working anymore. Her husband was the sole provider, and she had not been in the workforce for seventeen years because she'd stayed home to raise their kids. She knew things weren't great but was ultimately surprised when a divorce was proposed.

He made the money and also managed it. The good news was that he did a really good job of it.

Naturally, because she had been out of the workforce for a long time, she only had an IRA with her former employer worth about forty thousand dollars. Not much when retirement for her was only twenty years away. But because her soon-to-be ex had done a great job of saving, she knew she was going to get a nice amount of money as her half of his retirement savings, and she wanted to make sure she was doing the right thing. Something I've learned about women and their thought process is that most of us want to make sure that we are always "doing the right thing," no matter what the subject is. Money is no different. Tami and her ex were already several months into the divorce process, and final negotiations had started. She had already moved out of their family home.

Tami was and is so smart. She recognized that she needed help, but she didn't have the faintest idea of where to start. She knew she needed some education, and it was time to get serious about her situation and her new role as a sole decision maker when it came to her finances.

Tami appreciated that I took the time to educate her. You have to remember that she had made some decisions in the household when it came to the kids and household expenses when she was married, but beyond that ... nothing! Her ex had a large 401(k), had all the contingent savings accounts set up, and had been saving for the kids' college as well. At the time, she hadn't understood it or make any decisions about it, but she was confident that he had done a good job. She was pleasantly surprised but not shocked when her lawyer estimated that her share of the divorce proceeds equaled over $350,000 in retirement savings and about $80,000 in liquid cash savings. She was already in a good spot because her share of the property split was a decent sum, which she had already used to purchase her own new home.

For a most people, that is a lot of money to take possession of and start making decisions about! I have seen it go both ways. Women can be very good stewards of that money, but I have also seen them blow it all in a very short period of time. Like I said, in my practice I always start with education. Understanding how money works is an important building block to start making financial decisions. We were going to start with baby steps. This was going to be a long process because she was still in negotiations.

Part of the homework for both Tami and her lawyer was to create a budget to determine her alimony. We worked closely with her lawyer on those numbers to make sure her monthly maintenance would be appropriate for her new life. The other part was for her to start thinking about what she wanted her new life to look like.

Now that she was mentally getting ready to take on her new role and move forward as a part-time single mom, she was also ready to have some fun. She shared that it was her dream to be able to do some more traveling and have more experiences with her kids. Her ex was such a great saver that there wasn't a whole lot of fun to be had when they were married. She was ready to enjoy life—within reason, of course.

We started with her personal IRA. We were able to move her money into this super amazing indexed account that gave her an interest bonus of 7 percent, had great potential for growth, had absolutely no risk of market loss, had no fees whatsoever, and had the ability to provide an awesome income in retirement!

She definitely liked the sound of that. The other thing we put in place was a living benefits policy to protect her ability to make income; it would also protect all of her savings and retirement money in the event of a significant illness. We figured out her exact needs and determined an amount that was both appropriate and budget friendly.

Tami continued to come to Wine, Women and Wealth, and I could see how her confidence increased. She shared more, and her true self was coming out. She was amazing, beautiful, capable, and powerful! An awesome transformation was blossoming despite being in the midst of a hard life change. Sometimes as women, we just need to be given permission to allow ourselves to be the people we were meant to be. I really believe the encouraging, supportive women of our WW&W community was able to give that to her.

Tami spent some of her adult time up in the Colorado mountains. She had mentioned that she would love to buy some property in one of the resort towns up there. It was funny because she was asking my permission! Maybe *permission* is the wrong word; it was a mix of permission and advice. I told her that sounded like a great idea, and together we figured out how it would fit in her financial plan. Her oldest son could live in the condo and would pay rent to offset the cost. Plus, she would be building equity in another asset, and she could spend time there whenever she wanted! It was a total win! I am happy to report that she found a really great place and loves getting away to the mountains whenever she can.

The one thing that I always keep in mind is that it is the client's money, so I'm making their dreams and goals happen. I'm not here to tell them what to do; I'm here for perspective, education, and alternative options that could make more sense.

We still had more work to do. Tami had a sizeable chunk of money left over. We talked about her current position and what her future tax situation was going to look like. We came up with a comfortable number that she wanted to keep liquid for emergencies.

Once her cash reserves were in place, we still had forty thousand dollars left that she wanted to use for a more secure future. We were able to create a tax-free retirement fund that she never has to contribute to again if she doesn't want to. She already had a great deal of money that was growing tax deferred in her own IRA, as well as her share of her ex-husband's 401(k). I really wanted her to have some fun in retirement—and with tax-free money!

About a month and half later, her QDRO (Qualified Domestic Relations Order) was done, and there was a little more money ready to be disbursed. We talked about a couple of options. We could add to one of the accounts we'd already set up or start a new one. Because Five Rings is a non-fee-based company, we could make the decision based on Tami's needs rather than how much more it would cost to open a new account. We decided to open a new account to give her more flexibility when it came receiving retirement income later on. By layering, she could stagger when she drew income in the future in order to keep up with inflation or to provide for unforeseen wants or needs.

Even though we were able to help Tami land on her feet, the unfortunate truth is that this exact scenario happens all the time. Families aren't saving for the stay-at-home parent. Because they aren't making any "real" money, couples place little to no life insurance on that spouse who is staying home with the kids. They aren't making any "real" money, so they aren't funding their own

Roth or traditional IRA. But let's look at this a different way: even though they aren't making any "real" money, studies show that if anything was to happen to the stay-at-home spouse, it would cost anywhere from fifty to seventy thousand dollars per year to replace all that he or she provides to the family—things like childcare, tutoring, cooking, cleaning, and running a million errands. As a society, we are perpetually stuck in an old way of thinking about our money instead of looking at the whole picture. Breaking this cycle is our mission! We want to empower women to be more hands-on and participatory in the household finances. To be open to a new perspective is huge! As women, we need to be willing to stand up for ourselves as well as be great financial partners. It isn't selfish; rather, our input could be the perspective that protects the family the most.

Since Tami and I connected at that first Wine, Women and Wealth event, not only do we have an amazing client-counselor relationship, but I gained another girlfriend! We almost always see each other at our monthly WW&W gatherings. We are friends on Facebook, and we get to keep up with each other's busy lives. We call and text each other whenever we want to say hi. The blessings just keep on coming.

One of the best side effects of this business is watching people grow in their strength, knowledge, and confidence in money. Money is crazy. It can either benefit the other areas of your life or pull them down. Having a plan and knowing what your future looks like is incredibly empowering.

A few notes.

> Not all indexed accounts have a 7 percent bonus. They all vary. Remember that past performance doesn't guarantee future results. Your experience may be different depending on your personal plan.

KRISTEN JUDD

"There are so many reasons why I love Wine, Women and Wealth. It is my favorite night of the month. It is girl's night with a twist. You never know who you are going to meet -- who is going to change your life. You never know what you are going to learn. I learn something new every single month! You never know how you might have an opportunity to impact another person's life either by your words, your actions or even by helping someone like Tami set up her financial future with confidence."

A Little about Kristen

Kristen Judd has a degree in accounting and finance from Fort Lewis College in Durango, Colorado. After spending some time in corporate America and owning a couple of small businesses, she returned to financial services in 2014. Why? Because she found a company that focuses on financial education for individuals, families, and business owners. She has found her home and loves being able to be of service, whether it is her clients, fellow agents, or any of her team members. Kristen can relate to just about everyone's situation because she has experienced it. She is passionate about what she does. She especially enjoys giving people the opportunity to leave their financial strife behind and move forward with a plan they can believe in and grow with.

Kristen is the host of Wine, Women and Wealth in the Westminster, Colorado, area and has been giving back to that community since 2015. She is a dynamic and sought-after speaker for educational workshops and seminars. Last but not least, Kristen is the author of Own Your Future, a ninety-day journal to help you create your own future, realize your gifts and talents, achieve more goals, and live the life that you always saw yourself living. These are the actual steps she used to catapult her success with Five Rings Financial, and she would be thrilled if it could help you achieve your crazy big goals with ease and joy.

Robin

#MeToo

by Robin Kemp

I never thought I would have a career in the financial services industry. When I was growing up, my parents frequently discussed
the fact that they wanted me to become a doctor because of the
earning potential. But earning potential simply wasn't important
to me at the time. What does an eighteen-year-old know? I do
know that I chose not to become a medical doctor because of the
cost to become a doctor. The time, money, and the student loan
debt—no, thank you! I rebelled by going to college and receiving
a Bachelor of Arts degree in Communications instead.

When I graduated from college, I planned to have a lifelong
career in advertising. My first job out of college was at a small
advertising agency that specialized in promoting car dealerships,
and then I moved on to what I thought was my "forever" job.
My "forever" job gave me the opportunity to work on a national
marketing campaign and earn a sizable commission. It included
late nights with coworkers, going out for drinks after work, and
the chance to fit in with my new work family. Once, a group
of us bought tickets to see *The Phantom of the Opera* in Los
Angeles, and at other times we would have picnics at the beach.
I had fun with my work family. I loved my job, but this job also
included a boss who liked to snort cocaine and buy me lingerie
even though he was married. When the first pink and white box
from Victoria Secret appeared on my desk, I assumed it was

from my boyfriend, so I quickly lifted the lid off the box to find a sexy pink silk negligee with black lace trim. There was no note to indicate who had given me this lovely gift. I was holding it up by the delicate straps when my boss walked into my office.

He said, "That would look good on you."

Imagine that you are at the end of your life, and your whole life flashes before your eyes. A million thoughts raced through my head, mostly along the lines of, *How can I tell this man to f#@k off and still keep my job?*

Instead, I settled on a meek thank-you and slipped the limp fabric back into the box, put the lid back on, and smiled with all the demeanor I could muster to silently say to myself, *Not now, not ever.*

Don't worry, I won't tell, I thought to myself.

I was raised to be a good girl and do what I was told to do by a strict stepfather. I was not allowed to question authority growing up, so I put up with my boss and dismissed his behavior because "boys will be boys."

After all, this was my first real full-time job in my mid-twenties, and I was working with car salesmen. One time, a general manager of a Nissan dealership yelled at me in front of his staff about the project our agency was managing, and he threw a thousand-dollar check on the showroom floor just to humiliate me and watch me bend over to pick it up. I could barely contain the tears, but the general manager of that car dealership would never know how demeaning he was to me because I was determined to handle his boorish behavior on my own. On that particular day, one of the other salesmen followed me out to my car that day and asked if I was okay. I wasn't okay, but I lied and said, "I'm fine, thank you."

Although I felt like an integral part of my work family at my "forever" job, I did not have a close relationship with the owner of the company like my boss did. I knew I could not tell on my boss if I wanted to keep my job, my income, and my work family.

When I got married, my dysfunctional work family, including the owner, came to my wedding. I received generous gifts of cash, champagne flutes and dinnerware from my coworkers and we partied into the night. Two years later, when I got pregnant, my friends at my "forever" job threw me a baby shower. I felt the love when I received a hand-stitched green, yellow, and white blanket made just for my son. The day I returned from maternity leave, I was fired.

My "forever" job had lasted only four years. I was kicked out of my work family and was crushed. Suddenly, I was unemployed with a baby and a self-employed husband whose income could not make up for the loss of my earnings. This good girl was angry, and I started to question everything about my life. Having a baby and getting fired will do that to a person.

So, I decided to do something about it. I'm not allowed to talk about the details of the lawsuit, but I will say that I finally told someone about the terrible things that had happened to me. Losing my "forever" job was not the worst thing I'd ever experienced, but the *process* to sue a former employer was one of my worst experiences. I was made to recount every horrible and awful event that had ever happened to me from my earliest memory on, right up to my employment at my "forever" job, with as much detail as I could remember. My life had some untold secrets that I had tried to bury deep, so I didn't have to think about them. Now, not only was I made to dig up and think about my secrets, I was made to bring them to the surface and give life to the events that hurt my soul to say out loud. It seemed like the opposing counsel's strategy was to determine whether I had a habit of telling on people who treated me wrong and suing them. No wonder victims don't come forward. It was a slow, painful experience that almost broke me. We settled out of court the day before the trial.

I had won a settlement, lived through the telling of secrets, and survived a divorce. I was effectively "broken open." Turning thirty-three years old and living through that experience was a defining moment for me, one that shaped my thoughts and decisions about what my life would look like in the future.

For the first time, I started to formulate a plan and define what was important to *me*. It was my plan, not the plan of expectations that my family or society laid out for me.

My primary goal was simple: I was going to find a way to be my own boss. Nobody was going to have the power to fire me again unless it was a client.

My other goals included the following.
- Financial independence and *security*
- Being able to manage and *balance* my work and life
- Doing meaningful work that gives me a *purpose*

I quickly learned out of college that the people who really made money owned their own ad agency or they were in sales. An advertising career was cool and fun, but it was not meaningful.

Until I was fired, I had no idea what work-life balance meant. I began to look at other careers that might meet my goals.

Fortunately for me, my mom was an optician and entrepreneur who owned her own optical shop. Her store catered to the middle class and wealthy of Orange County, California, with quality eyeglasses that were a fashion statement. I had the great opportunity to work with her after I was fired and while my son was a baby. She would have been thrilled if I had wanted to take over the family business that she had created, but the opportunity did not meet all of my goals. It became impossible to bring my baby to work once he started walking, and I knew that I did not want to be a slave to a storefront and its hours.

So, I quit and moved through a series of jobs and opportunities that brought me to the insurance industry. *Hmm, that's interesting,* I thought to myself. *No little kid says, "I think I want to be an insurance agent when I grow up!"* But when I took a closer look, it seemed to meet my goals.

There were areas of insurance that I could focus on and grow as an independent business. I could be my own boss! I could work from home! If I worked hard, I could create my own financial independence and security with a residual income! I could become an expert and make a tremendous difference in people's lives! Check, check, check, and check!

However, now I needed to find the right insurance company. I was looking for a company that would mentor me and help me grow my business. It turned out that there were plenty of insurance companies willing to help me do that, and I was able to grow my own business as a broker. My business was close to meeting my goals, but something was missing. I felt like Prince

Charming in *Cinderella*, searching for the foot that would fill the glass slipper.

My friend Bobbi invited me to attend a Wine, Women and Wealth event at a cool wine bar in Carlsbad, California, to network and grow my business. I had been to plenty of other networking groups, but this was different from the moment I walked in. The energy in the room was vibrant and filled with women eager to make new friends and connect while sipping wine and enjoying cheese and crackers. Soon, a vivacious, twenty-something woman named Mara introduced herself to the room. Then she introduced the speaker, Denise, and the fact that Wine, Women and Wealth was like a book of the month club except you didn't need to read the book. I was relieved, sipped my wine, and listened as Denise asked the crowd, "If you had to pick a fairy tale that would describe your experience with money, which one would it be?"

I looked around the room and could see that the other women, like me, were eager to hear more.

After going over the fairy tale options, Denise continued by explaining, "Your money story, or what you believe is financially possible, has a bigger influence on your success than education, social advantage, or the right job."

I thought to myself, *I have never given any thought to what my beliefs are about money. I mean, sure, money doesn't grow on trees, but do I really believe that?*

Denise wrapped up her presentation by asking us to do a little homework and identify our money beliefs. Then she said, "If your money beliefs don't serve you, then write new ones." In fact, when we went around the room to introduce ourselves, we were asked to share a money belief with the other women in the room. There was an amazing sense of warmth and belonging. Yes, the wine was good, but the conversation was better!

I was hooked and decided to come to the monthly events. Over time, I realized what was missing from my own business and decided to work with Five Rings Financial as an independent representative. I discovered that Five Rings Financial had something that I had at my "forever job" all those years ago: a sense of community. Except this time, the culture of the company I choose to keep has integrity.

ROBIN
KEMP

"I love Wine, Women and Wealth because we can have vulnerable, heartfelt conversations about money without judgment. I love that I have the opportunity at the events I host each month to give women the space to do that. I love that we have built a community of women who look forward to these events every month and even bring their girlfriends because they know that we will welcome them."

....

A Little about Robin

Robin Kemp is a Senior Vice President with Five Rings Financial. She is a well-known speaker, hosting several monthly Wine, Women and Wealth events in Southern California and she produces and hosts a podcast by the same name. With over seventeen years of financial industry experience, Robin is committed to educating and helping middle-income Americans sleep well at night by protecting and growing their wealth. As such, she is the highly successful author of the book *Protect and Grow Wealth*, which outlines "Five steps to financial freedom so you can have a lifetime of income, a safety net and thrive."

Robin has raised three boys and currently lives in Carlsbad, California, with her husband and a rescue bunny.

Diane

"What Do YOU Want?
After All, It's YOUR Money"

by Denise Arand

I first met Diane in 2007 at a women's networking event. She's
an amazing artist and was there to meet a few other women
and to promote her beautiful ceramics. Diane is a very friendly
person, and we immediately hit it off. When I shared what I did
at Wine, Women and Wealth, she was excited to learn how we
work with people for long-range and retirement planning. She
said that she and her husband, Don, had been working with an
advisor for many years, but he'd moved away, and now they had
very little contact with him. They were concerned about some of
the financial instruments they had and wanted to be sure that
when retirement came, they were ready. One of their biggest
concerns was maximizing what they had already saved and making sure that they never again lost money in the stock market.

Here is Diane's story.

> At the time we met with Denise, Don and I had been
> married for twenty-two years and had been saving in
> our 401(k)s, IRAs, and other retirement plans. I had
> retired from a municipal job, so I had a small pension,
> which was great. Don worked at the local university,
> so he would also have a pension coming when he
> retired. We thought that we were pretty well set up,
> however we had suffered some significant losses when

the stock market crashed in 2000–2001, and we were worried that if the next downturn came right as we were planning to fully retire—or worse, right after we retired—then the money in our self-directed plans and 401(k)s would be diminished, and we would not be able to live the life we had planned in retirement. We never felt as though we were educated when it came to our finances, so we basically just followed the advice of our employers, our insurance agent, and the people we knew in real estate when we were buying or selling property.

We also hit a bit of a crunch because we owned three pieces of property. We were living in the dream home we had worked for so many years to own. We were excited to have this beautiful, new, 3,500-square-foot house in Southern California with a workshop where I could do my art, a study for Don and his computers, plus a lovely backyard with a meditation garden. We also still owned a home nearby, which had been our residence before we'd moved to the dream home. We had been advised by our realtor and our financial advisor at the time to hang on to that home and rent it out. Last but not least, we had also purchased a home near where our daughter was going to college. We rented rooms to some of her college friends and boarded horses on the property in order to offset the mortgage cost. We were able to qualify for the loan on these homes because of the very lenient financial guidelines of the time, and what the lender showed us that made it all work was an adjustable rate mortgage. We believed him when he said it was unlikely that the rate would ever go up, and if it did, we can always refinance because we would have equity, we would be able to get higher rents on the rental properties, and they would also be worth more.

This all worked pretty well until late 2007. We lost the tenants in the property that was our former residence, and we were having trouble renting it again. Our daughter had graduated from college, and the pool of renters we had from that university had dried up, so she was living there by herself with no other tenants to offset the mortgage. On top of that, the area was being rezoned to disallow horse stables on the property. We really hadn't considered that if we didn't have tenants, we would have to pay our mortgage, maintenance, property taxes, and property insurance on those houses out of our own budget! We also had the first adjustment on our adjustable loan on the dream house. Our loan rate went up significantly, which was really a sucker punch with all of the things going on with the other properties.

We found ourselves in a really scary financial position and sought out the advice of our financial advisor and insurance agent. He had been keeping us as a client as a "favor" because our liquid investable assets did not meet his minimum requirement of $250,000. When we were finally able to have a conversation with him, his advice was to walk away from our dream home and move back into our former residence. We had money and IRAs with him, however they were invested in mutual funds and had not done much in the way of growth, in spite of strong stock market returns in 2005–2007. We were a little bit disappointed in that because even though we would be unable to use that money to buy ourselves out of the real estate mess, it was money we were counting on using in retirement, and as I said earlier, we were fearful of losing it. The idea of walking away from our dream home broke our hearts, and the idea of just giving the property back to the bank went against any notion of good financial practices that we had ever heard. We had always gone by his advice and now were surprised to have him be so flippant when it came to our lives, dreams, and financial well-being.

We've always believed that whenever you have a serious medical diagnosis, you should always get a second opinion from another doctor. This seemed like a pretty serious financial diagnosis, so we sought out the advice of other financial representatives.

It was one of those "right place at the right time" things. I met Denise and we connected right away! I gave her a brief summary of our story; I was so comfortable sharing with her. We made an appointment for her to come and meet Don and me at our home. We were surprised when there was no big sales pitch; she simply asked us to summarize where we were at. When we told her about the plan that had been proposed to walk away from our dream house and move back into our old residence, she asked us a simple question. "What is it that *you* want?" That surprised us because, frankly, our financial advisor in the past had never asked us that question.

Don and Diane are typical Americans. They both have college degrees and great jobs, but they were never educated about how many really works. They were simply following the advice of their financial advisor, assuming he knew more than what they did about the best way to handle their money. What he didn't know, though, was what *they* really wanted.

First, we talked about their dreams and aspirations. Diane had already retired and was pursuing her "encore career" as a ceramic artist, which required space to create her pottery, sculptures, and jewelry; and included a potter's wheel and kiln. Having space for her studio in their home was a dream come true. Don was still working at the university and was looking forward to retiring in about ten years. The three kids were all grown, had completed college, and were relatively self-sufficient (although Diane hoped to tuck away some money to someday provide a wedding for each of her two daughters). Life had been pretty comfortable, and they had been able to travel a fair amount. Don had also been able to pursue his dream of restoring classic Mustangs. Their hope had been that in retirement, life would continue much as it had been all along, but Don would not have to trudge into work every day.

Then we talked about their current financial picture and what they had to work with to replace Don's income once he retired. It turned out that they had done a great job of saving for retirement. They also had set aside money in Diane's 401(k) that they had not yet touched. John also had a self-directed IRA from a previous university position and a Roth. Diane was already receiving a small pension from her municipal job, and Don expected a pension that would be nearly 80 percent of his income when he finally retired. They had also contributed to Social Security, and as long as it was still available when they reached the optimum age to take it, that would provide additional funds in retirement.

Their real problem existed *before* retirement! At that moment, as we were sitting at their dining room table, they had three mortgages, three sets of property tax and insurance, significant credit card debt from trying to keep up on all of those things, one property vacant, and one property under-rented. On top of that, the adjustable rate mortgage on their dream home had just increased, adding additional pressure to an already tight financial situation.

So, I asked the big question. "What is it that *you* really want? How would you like this to play out in a perfect world?" Their answer didn't surprise me. They wanted to keep their beautiful home. They didn't care to keep their former residence as a rental property. The college house where their daughter was living could also be sold once she found a new place to live. They would like to make sure that they were growing the money that they had in their retirement accounts wisely, because they didn't have time to recoup any losses should the stock market turn down again. And they were worried about what would happen when one of them passed away and the pension money stopped.

Now we were ready to 'refinance their finances'. Ever heard of refinancing a mortgage? You refinance a mortgage to reduce your payment and/or create capital, as well as to improve your financial situation. When you refinance your finances, you do the same thing: you take a look at your whole financial picture to bring down costs, increase returns, and in some cases create capital.

First, I introduced them to a realtor friend of mine, who sold the rental (their former residence). There was about $120,000 of equity in that home after closing costs, which they could use to payoff credit card debt and create a liquid savings account that could be used in case of emergency. Already, Don and Diane were sleeping better at night!

Next, my realtor friend determined that the college house unfortunately needed some work before it could be sold, and it didn't have enough equity to break even if they sold the property at that time. So, Don and Diane rolled up their sleeves, and every weekend for about three months, in true *Fixer-Upper* style, they rehabbed the property. They still couldn't sell it for enough to make sense, but they were able to find great tenants who offset the mortgage and insurance. Don and Diane still had to cover the property taxes, however the next year, the tenants loved the house so much that they purchased it—a win-win situation for all.

Then we tackled the retirement savings. Don and Diane always thought their mutual funds were doing fine. They rarely looked at their statements, figuring that the money would take care of itself. They noticed that their values dropped significantly in 2000 during the "Dot-Com Bubble Bust", however they felt powerless to change anything due to their lack of knowledge. So, they just kept contributing year after year by payroll deduction. Once Diane retired, her 403(b) funds stayed with the city for which she had worked. When we examined how much they had put into their accounts versus their current values, their net return was less than 4 percent over the last 10 years, which was probably due to the losses they'd sustained in 2001 and the fees they'd paid each year whether the market was up or down. They were pretty concerned that the next market downturn was coming. After all, it was 2007, and they had just recovered from their losses in 2001. We talked about the indexed accounts that go up when the market goes up and stay level when the market goes down. By moving their eligible funds (Diane's old 403(b) account and John's self-directed IRA) into this type of account, they were able to eliminate their fees, attain an immediate interest credit/bonus, and protect their money from further market risk. Why was this important? Because this was right before the market crash in 2008, and Don and Diane didn't lose a nickel—in fact, they came out ahead because they eliminated fees and got a 7 percent bonus on all the money they put into the account. (In this case, the bonus was 7 percent. Your own bonus may vary.)

Diane and Don learned some important lessons as we've worked together. First, if you get a serious diagnosis, whether about your health or your money, you should always get a second opinion. Second, always remember it's *your* money, and ultimately no advisor or agent has the right to tell you what to do with that money if it's not aligned with your goals. Third, as Warren Buffet says, "Rule Number One: Never lose money. Rule Number Two: See rule number one."

Throughout the years, Don and Diane have been awesome friends and clients. I look forward to getting together with them every year to review their accounts and to catch up on their lives. I was invited to Don's retirement party in June 2018, and I have to tell you that I was a little teary-eyed and very grateful that I had been able to play a little part in making that all happen. These days, they spend a lot of time with their seven grandkids. Their family is thriving, and they are enjoying the retirement years they had always dreamed of.

DENISE ARAND

"I always look forward to Wine, Women and Wealth nights! Little did I know how powerful it would be when the four of us had our very first meeting in 2007. Women love to connect, love to learn, and many want to know how to be more financially successful. I love that we provide a place where women can find community, learn about money, and be encouraged and uplifted."

A Little about Denise

Denise Arand began her financial services career in the 1990s, helping people plan for retirement the "old-fashioned" way, utilizing typical stock market investments. When she felt the pain of her client's unavoidable losses during the Dot-Com Crash of 2000–2002, Denise sought out ways help her clients build wealth with a reasonable return and *no* risk of market loss. Finding Five Rings Financial gave her access to those tools. Since signing on in 2006, she rose rapidly to the rank of Executive Vice President and spearheaded the expansion of Five Rings across the nation, beginning in California. Most of all, Denise is passionate about sharing proven, reliable financial advice to audiences who traditionally haven't access to it, especially women, middle-class Americans, and those who are looking for wealth-building alternatives to risky stock market investments.

As the proud founder of Wine, Women and Wealth, Denise is achieving her goals of educating and encouraging *all* women to be comfortable with money, personal finance, and building wealth. She's thrilled to see this message spread across the country as more and more Five Rings Financial representatives host WW&W events and empower more women.

Denise calls Carlsbad, California, home with her husband of forty-plus years. She's the mother of two very successful, married daughters and is "Mimi" to two beautiful granddaughters.

Annalise
The American Dream

by Heather Brinkman

I first met Annalise back in 2011. She was quiet and a bit timid, and she was German, which made her especially intriguing. She visited a weekly networking group that I attend, and I invited her to Wine, Women and Wealth. She was self-employed and was trying to meet people, as well as get clients for the nail business that she ran out of her home. She would also do her clients' nails in *their* homes, if needed, and that seemed kind of interesting to me. She was very pleasant, and we all liked her. We invited her back to visit again. She came often and became a wonderful addition to our community.

Annalise and I met for coffee several times over the next several months. She told me about her business and her dreams for the future. In turn, I shared with her what we do: retirement planning and protection for self-employed people, including one of my favorite things, tax-free retirement. She seemed interested but told me that her husband handled everything … and she seemed a bit concerned about that. As she started coming out of her shell, she joined us at Wine, Women and Wealth on a regular basis. This was a great match for her business: meeting more women! We all want to have great nails, don't we? She was also learning about money at Wine, Women and Wealth, and it was eye-opening for her. She even stood up and shared with our community of women, who had become her friends, her concerns of living in the United States and the way we do things here, compared to her country.

Here is Annalise's story.

I had never planned to permanently move to the United States. I had come to visit my sister, Gretchen, who went to school here and found a great job. I was just coming to visit for about six months. Gretchen loved Virginia Beach and said that I would too. She was right! I decided to take a class while I was here to learn some new techniques in the nail industry, which I had been doing back in my country for about five years before my visit. I thought, *Let me come to the United States, explore a bit, and maybe take a class or two but that's it. Then it's back to Germany, where my mom and dad are.* My sister worked long hours, but she had a friend whom she would get together with on a fairly regular basis. His name was Johnathan. The three of us hung out quite a bit, he loved our accents, and we all loved sharing stories and cooking together. For Gretchen, he was strictly a friend and nothing more. As for me and Johnathan, well, we fell in love. Johnathan knew I was only going to be here temporarily. That was my plan. With my time running out and my visa soon expiring, Johnathan asked me to marry him. At the time, I thought it was a great idea. We were in love! We flew back to Germany together so he could meet my family, I could tie up a few loose ends, and we could move my things to the United States.

When Johnathan and I got married, we ended up renting a home from his mother, who was not over-ly friendly with me. As much as I tried to build a relationship with her, it was useless. Even Johnathan wasn't close with her. I thought that was odd but didn't think much about it. In fact, Johnathan didn't seem to be close with anybody except me and my sister. We three still got together, but not as often as we had before. Gretchen was working a lot, and her job had her traveling more than she liked. As my business started growing and I was meeting and making new friends, Johnathan and I would often get asked out as a couple, but Johnathan never wanted to go; he just wanted to stay home. When we did go out, it was just the two of us, and sometimes my sister. We always went to the same places. That was not how I envisioned my life, my new marriage, and being in a new country.

My business was getting pretty good - it was really growing, and I even ended up renting a space for my clients to come to. I loved coming to Wine, Women and Wealth! Everyone was so welcoming. The wine was great, but mostly I enjoyed the information we received. I wanted to understand money. Things were very different in Germany. Our healthcare was taken care of and our social security system was quite good. I knew things were a bit different here, and I wanted to understand. I tried to speak with Johnathan about this as well. All he would tell me was that he had money that he was putting away in savings so that we could eventually buy our own home, and he also had a 401(k) through work. As many times as I asked, he would not give me any details. I wanted to understand because we shared the bills and the living expenses. I worried and kept doing as much as I could. I was in classes because I wanted to become an American citizen so that I could also know that someday, I would receive social security from the United States. I became a US citizen in the spring of 2013, and I was so excited! Becoming a US citizen also empowered me! I became more confident!

I contacted Heather. She had been so patient with me and was constantly trying to educate me about money, retirement, living benefits in case I got sick, and so much more. We had become really good friends over the last year and a half, and I did not hesitate to call her when I was ready. I wanted to know that I could put money away each month, but I also needed to know that my payment could be flexible in case of a bad month or two. She assured me that what we were doing was very flexible. She asked me how much I wanted to put away each month for my future. "My future"—that was a bit frightening. I had heard so many times (at Wine, Women and Wealth and from what I read online) that I needed at least a million dollars saved for retirement. I was concerned that I would never get there. Heather assured me that I would. She had a plan for me. She showed me how I could even add more money as my business grew. For the first time, I had a plan! I wouldn't have to be dependent on anyone else.

Heather set me up with what she called a tax-free retirement plan. I had heard about these at WW&W, so I understood it immediately. I started with two hundred dollars per month that I would pay into the plan. It even had living benefits in case I got sick and couldn't work, which was very important because I was self-employed. I didn't really say much to

Johnathan about my new plan. Every time I tried to speak to him about money or suggested that he should meet with Heather (or at least someone), he would get defensive and say no. I knew that now with my new plan, I was doing the right thing for *me*!

A little over a year later, Heather wanted to get together for my annual review. I was excited to see how well my plan was doing. My nail business was doing great as well. We discussed again the money I was putting in my plan. I told Heather that I wanted to put away an additional four hundred dollars per month. I was proud that my business was doing so well and that I could do that. I was living the American Dream! We talked over several ideas of how my money would work best for me and came up with a plan. Heather explained that we should use a little of that money for a term policy, which would protect me during my working years while I was building my retirement. It also had living benefits that would be a protection policy for me. This was money in case I got sick so that I didn't have to destroy my retirement plan. That seemed smart! After looking at several other options she showed me, I decided to start up an additional retirement plan (tax free with living benefits) because it made better sense to both of us. I will have two separate incomes coming in when I'm ready, and I can turn each of them on when the time is right. And best of all, if things go as planned, I will have $1.5 million saved by retirement! That's something I never could have dreamed of. I am so happy that I met Heather! She believed in me even when I didn't see it myself.

Since then, Johnathan and I bought a new home. It's beautiful and very serene because it sits on water and has very few neighbors. I still have my space I rent, but most of my clients now come to the house; it's their choice. I was finally able to get Johnathan to meet with Heather. She explained that because he now has a thirty-year mortgage, he needs mortgage protection. Like mine, it also has living benefits in case he gets sick and can't work, so he can continue to make the mortgage payments. If something happens to him, I can choose to stay in the house if I want. That has given me peace of mind! Johnathan and Heather had a good conversation about money—with me out of the room, of course. She says he's pretty stand-offish, but at least it's a start! We both hope he will open up with time, and not just about money.

A lot has happened since Annalise wrote that piece. Her marriage to Johnathan became unbearable for her. She was fed up and tired of walking on eggshells around him. She contacted me about a year ago and asked to meet me on a Sunday. We met at my office, and she looked miserable. She wanted to make sure her money was still doing well. I assured her that indeed everything was right on track. She told me that she needed help and didn't know who to turn to. It became clear to me why we were meeting before she even said anything: she needed my advice. She decided that she had had enough and was leaving Johnathan. We had a long talk and spoke about her options. I was able to refer her to law group that works with only women. She was relieved about that. It is nice to know that our clients, our friends, trust us with everything. We are their confidants! It's an honor that we don't take lightly.

Another year has passed. Even though Annalise has tried to make it work with Johnathan, her love for him has gone. It looks like their marriage can't be salvaged at this time, and they are talking divorce. There are so many moving parts with this. The silver lining is that Annalise is building her *own* tax-free retirement pension. She has her *own* living benefits plan. She has options, and she doesn't need to rely on anyone but herself.

Today, Annalise is an amazing, confident woman and business owner, and she is truly living the American Dream. She is an inspiration to all who know her and a wonderful part of our Wine, Women and Wealth community. I am so thankful to have her in my life as a friend and client, and I am so happy that we were able to create a foundation for her by establishing her own financial plan! As I always say, life is unscripted, but your peace of mind can be. Annalise is a perfect example of this, and it's why I love what I do. I'm so proud to play a positive part in people's lives.

HEATHER BRINKMAN

"Wine, Women and Wealth is what really hooked me into this business. That first event I attended was so eye-opening! I thought about my parents: my dad handled all of the money, and my mom never knew anything about it. When he passed away, she had no idea what to do and was so lost. I don't ever want another woman to go through that.
I love that Wine, Women and Wealth empowers women to learn about money, be smart about money, and be brave about money."

A Little about Heather

Heather Brinkman has an extensive, thirty-year background in the world of finance as a mortgage loan officer, mortgage closing agent, property tax management consultant, and business and group benefits specialist. Heather is a military spouse and has been self-employed for the last twenty-three years.

Since 2011, Heather has enjoyed an exciting and rewarding career as an Executive Vice President and Safe Money Advisor with Five Rings Financial. With hundreds of lifelong clients throughout seventeen states in America, Heather is helping families and small business owners accumulate, protect, and distribute wealth in safe, smart, and effective ways. She especially enjoys educating and empowering women about money, and the Wine, Women and Wealth program has played a pivotal role in her success.

Heather lives in Virginia Beach with her husband and her golden retriever, Annie.

Emily
"It's Time to Own My Future"
by Susan McCormick-Davis

Emily is a forty-something divorced teacher who I got to know at church. Over time, we became good friends. She has three daughters, two were in elementary school when we first met. We bonded over our love of all kinds of music -- especially show tunes! As we got to know each other better, she shared with me her goal of becoming more empowered about her personal finances and being a great example to her daughters. I invited Emily to Wine Women and Wealth so she could meet other like-minded women who were empowering themselves by learn-ing about how to have more financial success. That's one thing I love about Wine, Women and Wealth: we build these amazing communities of women who support and encourage each other.

Here is Emily's story.

> After my divorce four years ago, I really felt beaten down. As a doctor, my ex-husband earned a lot of money, however we could never hold onto it. He believed in real estate and so bought a ton of it. He even invested in a "cannot lose" real estate project in Panama, and guess what? We lost it all. Of course, he didn't tell me until it was too late. I guess it's true that opposites attract because I'd always been a saver. Fortunately, during our marriage, I was pretty good

at saving in my retirement accounts, funding them directly from my paycheck.

When the divorce was over, I placed some of my settlement funds at a local brokerage firm. I was so worn out that I frankly wasn't that careful. It felt good to have my own money, and I could decide where I would spend it. There were lots of dinners out and a few vacations after the divorce just to make myself feel better. I rented an apartment close to my kid's school. I put any planning on the back burner and focused on my music and my career; I teach music and math. I also took up martial arts classes to get physically stronger.

But then reality set in. My ex pays alimony and child support—sometimes! I have to constantly pursue him to pay late and skipped payments. It's exhausting and expensive to have my attorney involved. I finally realized that it was time for me to step up and take control of my own finances so I wouldn't have to depend on him forever.

I was ready to own my future financial stability, but really didn't know where to start. As a teacher, I've always felt funny that I didn't know more about investing, but I soon found out that none of my teacher friends really paid close attention to investing either. My natural "go-to" resources were all in the same boat as me.

When Susan and I became friends and I learned more about her background, I felt I could trust her. I was ready to get serious about my financial future and my kids' college funds. She invited me to Wine, Women and Wealth. It was so comforting to meet so many women in a similar position. I also loved learning about money from a woman's perspective. The more I attended, the more I realized I could "own" my financial future and create what I wanted. So, I asked Susan if she could talk privately with me about what I could do for myself and my kids.

When Emily learned that I help families plan for their financial security, she asked if we could sit down to talk further about what could be done for the younger girls' college funding, and if I could check her retirement plans. As is my practice, we reviewed Emily's current situation at our first meeting and talked about how she wanted her future to look.

Her current situation was certainly not the worst story I've heard. She had managed to save in her 403(b) plan at work and would receive alimony for life (as long as she never remarried). There were some funds in a 529 college funding plan for her daughters. Emily has a pretty good income as a highly acclaimed teacher, so it was good to have the cash flow for basic expenses. Her income was consistent, however she felt burned out with teaching.

One of the biggest challenges Emily faced was that her ex-husband kept bouncing around from job to job, so sometimes months went by with no alimony or child support coming in. Then it was a battle to get him caught up again. She felt upset because the inconsistent alimony and child support kept putting her in debt while she waited for the next judgment.

The bottom line was that Emily felt unprepared for the future. She wanted to give her kids a good start in life with money for college. She really wanted to save to buy a house in her dream town. She wanted to retire someday. And she was eager to learn and become as she put it "a student of how money really works".

Because Emily had some unpredictable financial factors in her life, we started with what she *could* control. She *could* decide on her own budget and live on that money. Her parents had been very frugal, and she'd learned about budgets from an early age. She *could* review how her 403(b) funds were invested and become educated in what fit her future best. Emily *could* also learn how 529 plans worked to decide whether this was best for saving for her daughters' college funding.

We created a plan that was serious about meeting Emily's future goals. We started with her retirement income goals. She wanted to have about $100,000 a year and felt she had about twenty years to save to create that income stream. She had already put over $200,000 away in an IRA rollover from an earlier corporate job, so we started there. She wasn't sure how it was invested in her brokerage account, so she met with her advisor. She was less than pleased to find out that over four years, in one of the strongest bull markets in history, her account had averaged less than 4 percent in annual returns after fees! We were able to transfer those funds with no tax ramifications into an account that would have reasonable return during years when S&P 500 had positive returns, but it would never lose when the S&P lost value. Best of all, there are no fees.

Next, we looked at the 403(b) plan that she had as a teacher. While she's employed by the school district, those funds already invested in the 403(b) must remain in that plan, however she could simply choose to stop contributing to it. She could then "re-direct" those funds to create her own tax-free retirement plan, which grows tax-deferred and then can create tax-free income in the future. It's one of my favorite tools when helping people plan. We met several times to work out how much she would need to save now for her goal of $100,000 in annual income in the future, and she realized by putting $600 a month into this plan, she could achieve her goal! As for that dream home, she could take a tax- and penalty-free distribution from this plan in about ten years for her down payment.

For her children, Emily decided to use that same type of tax-free plan to build up their college funding. One thing she loves is that this plan is so flexible that her kids aren't required to use it for education; they can use it to start a business, pay for a home down payment, or simply save it for their own retirement. There are so many options. Emily is really looking forward to teaching her kids to how to own their future too!

Emily feels so much better about her future now. Her financial stability isn't constrained by her ex-husband's financial ups and downs. Her daughters have a great example to follow of a woman in control of her own financial future. She is making her dreams come true.

SUSAN McCORMICK-DAVIS

"After I left my career with Wall Street firms, I searched for a financial group that really was empathetic to the many women who feel underserved and uneducated about money. When I was invited to a San Diego Wine, Women and Wealth meeting, I knew something was different from the buzz in the air that night. Women were introducing themselves and getting to know each other over a glass of wine. Everyone was so friendly and open. After about thirty minutes, we were encouraged to take a seat, and all attention was focused on an attractive, smiling woman commanding the front of the room. She introduced herself as Denise Arand, the founder of Wine, Women and Wealth. She let us know what to expect and encouraged us to find one new woman from the group we could have coffee (or wine) with, get to know, and see how we could help each other. The presentation was a chapter from a book about how to improve your relationship with money. It was so relevant, and I could tell from their reactions that everyone took away something positive from her talk. Next, we got to hear from every woman in the room—so many interesting and dynamic women.

Many came each month, and some were brand-new to the group. By the end of that meeting, I knew Wine, Women and Wealth was something really special—a safe place where women are encouraged to learn more about money from a female point of view. Wine, Women and Wealth, created with such love by Denise Arand, is a sisterhood of those empowered women!"

A Little about Susan

Susan McCormick Davis is an influencer in Personal Financial Education and is especially focused on empowering women in their relationships with money. She was a senior manager on Wall Street, but after thirty years, she left to teach the most important fact in success with personal finances: never lose money.

In 2014, Susan joined Five Rings Financial, an amazing company making a profound and positive impact on America. Susan joined this team of financial professionals to best assist her clients in accomplishing their personal and retirement goals. Susan seeks to educate her clients first on the options available for meeting their financial objectives. She then assists them in making more informed decisions and ultimately creates a customized plan for their particular situation. She enjoys hosting her monthly Wine, Women and Wealth events in San Diego and Orange County.

Susan is a native Californian who now lives in San Diego with her husband. Yoga is her passion.

Sarah
Pay Your "Old Lady" First

by Kim Harrison

A few years ago, I met a lovely young lady at a luncheon hosted by a mutual friend. We were discussing a service project for the community, and Sarah had just returned from a mission trip in Israel. She was bright eyed and full of enthusiasm. I was attracted to her energy right away and really wanted to get to know her. I like hanging out with positive people! I learned that she was a licensed cosmetologist and because my current hair stylist was moving away, I was in the market for a new one. I made an appointment with Sarah.

I was right about her energy, and through our time together, I learned a bit about her. She was twenty-three years old and loved helping people. Her parents were divorced, and her mom was remarried to a doctor. Sarah's mom was also being treated for breast cancer and was in the fight of her life. At the time I met her, Sarah was living with her mom and stepdad, helping to take care of her mother, both physically and emotionally.

As always happens with me, the conversation eventually came around to Wine, Women and Wealth. I invited Sarah to join us. At first, she was not really interested, but after several months of hair appointments, she finally decided that she would give it a try.

Sarah considered herself to be shy, and she felt a little awkward in crowds, but because of the warm and inviting atmosphere at our events, the minute she walked into the room, she felt comfortable. She sat at a table with three women all older than she, but she smiled and had a good time. I noticed that she was also networking. This was fantastic because at the time, she was just getting started in the business and did not have a lot of repeat clientele. Little did I know, Sarah learned a lot that night.

Sarah's story.

> Growing up, my sisters and I always had to beg for what we wanted. There was enough money for food and such but never any extra. I always felt like money was a thing I would never have enough of. When I was older and in high school, my mom married a man with lots of money, but it still felt as if we didn't have enough. I was too shy to ask because often as a younger girl, I was told, "No, we don't have the money for that." I worked and paid my own way through cosmetology school, and that was a good feeling. As soon as I started working, I thought I would be raking in the dough, but I still found myself just scratching by. I had two roommates just to make ends meet, yet most of the time, I still came up short.
>
> Then my mom got sick. I was devastated. I was so afraid that I would lose her to the cancer, and I wanted to be close to her every minute I could to take care of her. I am the oldest daughter and I felt it was my responsibility to be there for her. My stepdad was always working, so I moved in with them so Mom

wouldn't be alone so much. It also helped me to save money because I was still struggling financially.

I'm so glad to report that my mom beat cancer and is in great health now. Even though it was such a hardship, I am so grateful for the time I was able to help her. I learned a lot during that time, especially that life is something worth fighting for. I know that it cost a lot of money for her treatments, and I will always be grateful that my stepdad was able to take care of that for her. I am sure if she had not had him, her recovery would have been more stressful due to the lack of money and the worry she would have for us. I also know that I would have spent every penny possible to pay for her treatments. None of us had to do that.

When Kim invited me to Wine, Women and Wealth, I felt like it was not for me. I was flat broke, and the only thing I knew about wealth was that I didn't have it or know anything about it. I thought I would feel stupid in front of these women who had it all figured out. I was also really struggling to find new clients and thought that taking the time away from my mom for an evening was not a good idea. Boy, was I wrong! Kim kept inviting me and encouraging me. She finally convinced me when she said that the ladies in the group had been complimenting her on her hair and that if I came, I might be able to get a few more clients. So, I decided to get over my fear and go see what it was all about.

I immediately felt at home because Kim met me at the door and right away introduced me to a few people who were very nice. I was less nervous. But the thing that changed everything for me was when I learned that I was not alone in thinking that I never had enough money. I learned about scarcity thinking and how it affects my ability to create more of what I want. My scarcity mind-set was actually creating more scarcity in terms of money! I learned that I could change my thinking and create more financial abundance. I was so excited to know that I could do it and that I was not the only one who thought this way. When I introduced myself to the group, I was surprised at how confident I sounded, and that night I attracted three new clients who are still my regular customers. I was thrilled!

After some time attending WW&W and talking with Kim, I felt that I could not only make money but also have some left over. I could actually save money! She showed me that at my age, little bits of money put away earning a decent interest rate, and over time that could net me a big pile of money. She encouraged me to "pay my old lady first." She said, "Someday, you will be old. You will have needs, and if you take care of her now, your 'Old Lady' will thank you." I got it. I started a plan with only fifty dollars a month. She told me that over time, I could add more money as I earned more, and that is exactly what I have done. I now feel so grown-up and responsible. By saving money in this way, I am taking care of myself.

This little habit has changed so much for me. I have a thriving business as a stylist with plenty of regulars, I am married, and I have bought a house. My husband has also started a plan to save for his retirement that is separate from what he is contributing at work. It really isn't impacting our newlywed lives much. We sometimes order pizza instead of going out for date night, but we are proud of the choices we are making to take care of our future today.

At our first annual review, Sarah decided that she was able to contribute more on a monthly basis to her retirement account. She also asked some questions about how living benefits work and whether they might be a good thing for her. Because of the experience she went through with her mom, she knew firsthand how expensive cancer treatment can be, and if she were to have something like that happen to her, she and her husband would not have the resources to make up the remaining costs after health insurance paid for its part. Because she was self-employed, Sarah realized that if she was unable to work, their income would be cut in half, and considering they now had a mortgage payment, she was not comfortable with that scenario. We added a living benefits plan for both her and her husband so they could sleep better at night.

As Sarah shared, she has learned many things from attending Wine, Women and Wealth.
- She is not the only person who struggles with money issues.
- Our mind-set can cause a feeling of lack when it comes to money.
- Women are supportive and want to help each other grow wealth.
- There is a way to start small when it comes to investing, and as she earns more, she can save more.

Sarah now tells everyone about Wine, Women and Wealth and invites them to join her. She even keeps a couple of invitations at her stylist station so people in her chair can inquire about it, and she can share the gift of financial freedom. She is still my stylist, and I still get lots of compliments on my hair.

KIM HARRISON

"I feel so blessed to work with people like Sarah and to help her see that her past history with money didn't need to predict her financial future. I love helping people rewrite their money stories to create a happy ending. Because of our warm, welcoming, and frankly, fun environment at Wine, Women and Wealth, we are able to engage people who might never seek the financial advice that could make huge difference in their lives."

A Little about Kim

Kim attended her first Wine, Women and Wealth in November 2011. She immediately saw the magic and brilliance of the marketing dynamic and was hooked. She found Wine, Women and Wealth because she was looking to launch a new career. As an academic success coach, she was transitioning from the public education sector to private practice and thought that Wine, Women and Wealth was a great place to begin her search for connections with women in the community. Little did she know that she would go through a transition of her own over the next few years. Wine, Women and Wealth became an important part of her business and personal life, and by 2014 she was co-facilitating a monthly event. She left her private practice and coaching business in 2016 to join her husband at Five Rings Financial. Together, they have built a successful agency in Western Colorado and Nevada. She continues to facilitate a monthly Wine, Women and Wealth in Grand Junction, Colorado, and has launched events in multiple locations in Colorado, Nevada, Idaho, and Oregon. Her desire to build a community of women who lift each other up and gain education about financial wealth together while creating relationships of value is what brings her the most professional fulfillment.

Kim, under the name K. L. Harrison, is the author of *Grandma's Money Tree*, a book designed to illustrate the importance of adults saving for their children and their children's children. This short read is great for young children because it uses a fictional "money tree" to visually depict family members who set aside money for children when they are young, in order to have a mature "crop" that is ready to be used once the child grows up.

What Now?

I've heard it said, "If you want to change something in your life, you're probably going to have to change something in your life." That couldn't be truer when it comes to dealing with your finances. Although change isn't always the easiest thing to do, if you always do what you've always done, you'll always get what you've always gotten. The women you've met in the previous pages did just that. They faced their fears, took charge, and made the changes necessary to create their own financial success.

I hope you've found the women in our Wine, Women and Wealth community relatable and maybe even a little like you or someone you know. Sometimes just knowing that someone like you is winning the money game can be comforting, even energizing! If learning about them stirred in you a little desire to create more financial success in your own life, then here are a few steps to get you there.

> **Before you do anything, consider your money mind-set.** How do you feel about money? Do you have a lot of limiting beliefs about money, like "Money doesn't grow on trees" or "Money is the root of all evil"? Perhaps that limiting belief isn't about money—it's about yourself. Do you think you're worthy of financial success? Either way, your first step is fixing your "relationship" with money. There are more great books in the resources section at the end of this book

to help you improve your money mindset. Or come to a Wine, Women and Wealth event in your area, if there is one. This money mind-set is something we talk about all the time, and we are some of the most positive people you'll ever meet.

Next, assess your current situation. Really take a good, hard look. Do you know how much you're spending versus what you're bringing in? What's your debt situation? Do you have a savings account set aside with liquid funds "just in case..."? How about saving for your future, such as college for your kids and your own retirement? (I know sometimes these things are hard to look at. That's why we like wine.) What's working, and what keeps you up at night? It's important to really, really, really know your whole financial picture. Whether you like what you see, or you don't, there's no way to know how to move forward until you complete this step. There are lots of tracking and budgeting resources online. I like Mint (https://www.mint.com/) if your finances aren't too complicated. Again, check out the resources section at the end of this book.

Now it's time to dream ... to look into the future. Financial success, especially retirement, isn't guaranteed – you have to plan for it. So, you might as well plan it the way you want it. What does retirement look like for you? At what age? Will you keep working just because you want to, because you love what you're doing? Will you create an "encore career" – doing something because you've always wanted to? Will you travel? Will you finally just have the time to garden, to craft, to read? Is volunteering in your future? Write it all out – just the way you want it to be. If you change your mind, then guess what? The pen is in your hand – you have the power to rewrite your own happy ending.

Here's something to think about as you are pondering your retirement

One of the most inspirational women I know is eighty-plus years old and continues her work as a piano teacher. She has thirty students every week, singlehandedly puts on a recital and reception every month, dresses fabulously, and always has her hair and makeup perfectly done. She is an officer in the state music teachers' association and travels to her students' performances whenever possible. She's sharp as a whip and in pretty great shape physically. She could have easily retired twenty years ago. I've asked her a couple of times if she's thinking about retiring yet, and her reply is always, "Well, honey, then why would I get up in the morning?" She has purpose. She has passion. And that keeps her young and vital.

Once you've completed these steps, it's time to build your team. First and foremost, you'll need a licensed financial professional. The strategies we've talked about in this book must be facilitated through a financial professional. It's important to find someone who listens to you, responds to your needs, and answers questions directly. It should be someone who has a solid company with a great reputation behind him or her. It should be someone you can trust. Get to know the person you are working with. Trust your gut. Get references. Check their track record.

Throughout this book, I've tried hard to make sure it doesn't sound like a "commercial" for Five Rings Financial. Now that you know our story, who we are and what we stand for, I hope you understand that we can help you too. That being said, if you don't meet with a Five Rings representative, choose someone who is aligned with your aspirations and can provide you with the road map to reach the dreams and goals you've set for yourself. Find someone who will treat you with respect no matter how much (or how little) money you are starting with. Also, very important, be sure to know their fee structure.

If you seek out advice from other companies, advisors, or representatives, be aware that they may give you very different advice than you've seen on these pages. That's simply a difference of opinion - it doesn't necessarily make our strategies right and theirs wrong, or vice versa. Just as there are lots of opinions about how to raise your kids, how to make the best lasagna, or whether Ford, Toyota, or Mercedes make the best cars, there are lots of opinions about how to grow wealth. Keep getting educated and understand what works best for *you* - Remember, it's *your* money!

Once you have chosen the financial consultant you'd like to work with, ask for recommendations for the rest of your wealth-building team. Depending on how complicated your finances are, you may need either a tax accountant or CPA, possibly a bookkeeper, or an estate planning attorney. As your relationship grows (as well as your wealth), your advisor may recommend other services and providers to pave your path to financial success.

Maybe you just need to make a little adjustment – things aren't bad, they just aren't as good as you'd like them to be. Maybe you need a whole financial makeover. Whatever you do, take action! Your new Wine, Women and Wealth girlfriends want you to know that although money might not buy happiness, lack of money makes life a lot harder, especially as you age. It's never too late to have a happy ending. You're never too old (or too young) to get started. No situation is hopeless. Always remember that it's *your* money. It's time to take control of your finances, your life, and your happiness. We are here for you on your journey. Cheers to your financial success!

Glossary

As you travel the road to financial success, you may stumble upon words that aren't used in everyday language. We've tried to avoid the use of financial lingo in this book, but just so you don't get tripped up, here are some definitions to some of the commonly used words of "financial-ese" …

401(k) - A 401(k) plan is a qualified employer-sponsored retirement plan offered by private employers that eligible employees may make tax-deferred contributions from their salary or wages to on a post-tax and/or pretax basis. Employers offering a 401(k) plan may make matching or non-elective contributions to the plan on behalf of eligible employees and may also add a profit-sharing feature to the plan. Earnings in a 401(k) plan accrue on a tax-deferred basis, however withdrawals are generally taxed as ordinary income.

403(b) - A 403(b) plan is a qualified employer-sponsored retirement plan much like a 401(k) but offered by government employers and tax-exempt organizations.

457 plan - A 457 is a qualified employer-sponsored retirement plan much like a 401(k) but offered to state and local public workers, as well as executives at nonprofit organizations

529 plan - A 529 plan is a tax-advantaged savings plan designed to help pay for education. Originally designed to pay post-secondary education costs, it was expanded to also cover K-12 education

Annuity - An annuity allows a customer to place money with an insurance company that can earn interest and grow on a tax-deferred basis with the opportunity to draw a stream of income in the future for a specific period of time, including lifetime.

Bear Market – A bear market is a condition in which securities prices fall 20% or more from recent highs amid widespread pessimism and negative investor sentiment. Typically, bear markets are associated with declines in an overall market or index like the S&P 500, but individual securities or commodities can be considered to be in a bear market if they experience a decline of 20% or more over a sustained period of time - typically two months or more.

Bull Market – A bull market is the condition of a financial market of a group of securities in which prices are rising or are expected to rise. The term "bull market" is most often used to refer to the stock market but can be applied to anything that is traded, such as bonds, real estate, currencies and commodities. Because prices of securities rise and fall essentially continuously during trading, the term "bull market" is typically reserved for extended periods in which a large portion of security prices are rising. Bull markets can last for months or even years.

Compound interest – Interest that is calculated on the principal amount and also on the accumulated interest of previous periods, and can thus be regarded as "interest on interest". It is most commonly calculated in daily, monthly, semi-annual and annual periods.

Death Benefit - A death benefit is a payout to the beneficiary of a life insurance policy or annuity when the insured or annuitant dies. Generally, named beneficiaries receive the death benefit as a lump sum and are usually not subject to income tax.

Disposable income - Disposable income, also known as disposable personal income (DPI), is the amount of money that households have available for spending and saving after income taxes have been accounted for.

Dow Jones Industrial Average - The Dow Jones Industrial Average (DJIA) is an index that tracks 30 large, publicly-owned companies trading on the New York Stock Exchange and the NASDAQ.

Emergency fund - An emergency fund is a readily available source of assets to help one navigate financial dilemmas such as the loss of a job, a debilitating illness, or a major repair to your home or car. The purpose of the fund is to improve financial security by creating a safety net of cash or other highly liquid assets that can be used to meet emergency expenses, as well as reduce the need to draw from high-interest debt options, such as credit cards or unsecured loans—or undermine your future security by tapping retirement funds.

Encore career - An encore career is term describing a second vocation in the latter half of one's life, popularized by author and social entrepreneur Marc Freedman. An encore career is typically one that is pursued as much for its purpose and for the sense of fulfillment it provides as for a paycheck.

Indexed accounts – an indexed account is a term used to describe a tax-deferred, long-term savings option that provides principal protection in a down market, with a zero-loss floor and opportunity for growth in an up market, generally subject to a cap or participation rate. Indexed accounts are not invested in stocks or mutual funds, rather they are held in an account that is credited interest based on the performance of a stock index like the S&P500.   They are designed for long-term goals. Indexed accounts, should not be confused with indexed mutual funds.

Indexed funds - An index fund is a type of mutual fund with a portfolio constructed to match or track the components of a financial market index, such as the S&P 500, Dow Jones Industrial Average or NASDAQ. These funds follow their benchmark index no matter the state of the markets, therefore are subject to market gains and risk of loss.

IRA - A traditional IRA (individual retirement account) allows individuals to self-direct pre-tax income toward investments that can grow tax-deferred. The IRS assesses no capital gains or dividend income taxes until the beneficiary makes a withdrawal, at which time, the withdrawal is generally taxed as ordinary income.

Life insurance - A life insurance policy is a contract with an insurance company. In exchange for premium payments, the insurance company provides a lump-sum payment, known as a death benefit, to beneficiaries upon the insured's death. There are many different kinds of life insurance, some permanent and some for a certain period of time.

Living benefits are additional benefits associated with some life insurance and annuity solutions provided by optional riders. Based on the product, living benefits can accelerate life insurance death benefits should a qualifying terminal, chronic or critical illness or critical injury occur to provide financial relief during that time. These benefits are generally paid directly to the owner of the policy and are generally not subject to income tax.

Long Term Care Insurance - Long-term care insurance is coverage that provides nursing-home care, home-health care, personal or adult day care to individuals with a chronic or disabling condition that needs constant supervision. Long term care benefits are generally paid directly to the provider, either a skilled nursing facility or home health care provider.

Million Dollar Baby Plan – a college and life funding plan for children under the age of 18 that utilizes instruments that accumulate and grow after tax dollars to create a plan that will distribute tax free for college and if maintained, can provide life insurance, living benefits and possible tax-free retirement for life.

Money 101 is a Five Rings Financial educational workshop that covers financial principals that can be utilized to grow and protect money for college funding, retirement or simply wealth building. Not to be confused with a sales seminar, there are no products sold at this event

Money Mind-set, Money Relationship, Money Self-Talk, Money Soundtrack – Are the thoughts, feelings and opinions that one has about their finances. It really drives how you make financial decisions every day. If you change your mindset, self-talk, and/or soundtrack you will change your relationship with money and ultimately make better choices about your personal finances.

Money Mommy and Me – a Five Rings Financial educational workshop that focuses on educating adults about how to teach their children , from age 3 to 21, basic money principals. This is a complementary workshop, and despite the name, dads, grandparents or anyone with a young person in their lives are welcome.

NASDAQ - Nasdaq is a global electronic marketplace for buying and selling securities, as well as the benchmark index for U.S. technology stocks. Most often, the term, "Nasdaq" is used to refer to the Nasdaq Composite, an index of more than 3,000 stocks listed on the Nasdaq exchange that includes the world's foremost technology and biotech giants such as Apple, Google, Microsoft, Oracle, Amazon, and Intel.

Networking - Networking groups usually meet weekly or monthly for the primary purpose of exchanging referrals. Meetings include open networking; short presentations by everyone; a longer, more detailed presentation by one or two members; and time devoted solely to passing business referrals.

Pension – A pension plan is a type of retirement plan where an employee adds money into a fund that includes contributions by the employer. The worker's pension payments are determined by the length of the employee's working years and the annual income they earned on the job leading up to retirement.

QDRO/Qualified Domestic Relations Order - The QDRO is the judicial order outlining the property division in a divorce or legal separation. Pensions, and retirement plans such as 401(k), 403(b) or 457 plans, IRAs may be included in the property division, as well as federal and state civil service plans.

Rollover - An individual retirement account rollover is a transfer of funds from a qualified retirement account, such as 401(k), 403(b) or 457 plans into a traditional IRA or a Roth IRA. This can occur through a direct transfer or by check, which the custodian of the distributing account writes to the account holder who then deposits it into another IRA account. In most cases, as long as the rollover is completed within 60 days, there is no taxable event.

Roth IRA - A Roth IRA is a retirement savings account that allows your money to grow tax-free. You fund a Roth with after-tax dollars, meaning you've already paid taxes on the money you put into it. In return for no up-front tax break, your money grows tax free, and when you withdraw at retirement, you receive a tax-free distribution.

S&P 500 - The S&P 500 or Standard & Poor's 500 Index is a market-capitalization-weighted index of the 500 largest U.S. publicly traded companies. The index is widely regarded as the best gauge of large-cap U.S. equities, as well an excellent barometer of the health of the American economy.

Social Media - Social media refers to websites and applications that are designed to allow people to share content quickly, efficiently, and in real-time. The ability to share photos, opinions, events, in real-time has transformed the way we communicate, gather information and the way we do business. Specific examples referenced in this book include Facebook, LinkedIn, and Meetup, although there are many more.

Stock index - A stock index or stock market index is a measurement of a section of the stock market. It is computed from the prices of selected stocks (typically a weighted average). It is a tool used by investors and financial managers to describe the market, and to compare the return on specific investments. Some examples are the Dow Jones Industrial Average, the S&P 500, or the NASDAQ Composite, although there are many more obscure indices.

Stock market - The stock market refers to the collection of markets and exchanges where regular activities of buying, selling, and issuance of shares of publicly-held companies take place. Such financial activities are conducted through institutionalized formal exchanges or over-the-counter (OTC) marketplaces which operate under a defined set of regulations. There can be multiple stock trading venues in a country or a region which allow transactions in stocks and other forms of securities.

Tax-deferred - Tax-deferred status refers to earnings on principal such as interest, dividends, or capital gains which accumulate tax-free until the owner takes constructive receipt of the profits. The most common types of tax-deferred instruments include individual retirement accounts (IRAs) and deferred annuities.

Tax-free or tax-exempt strategy – A tax-free strategy utililizes after-tax dollars, grows tax-deferred and then may be distributed tax-free/tax-exempt. Certain financial instruments, including Roth IRAs, Municipal Bonds and some types of permanent life insurance may function in this manner.

Tax-free retirement – A phrase popularized by best-selling author Patrick Kelly in his books "Tax-Free Retirerment" and "The Retirement Miracle". This concept is outlined in detail in these books and is a cornerstone of the education strategy of Five Rings Financial.

Traditional IRA - The traditional IRA is the most common type of IRA. It allows individuals to save for retirement with pre-tax dollars that grow tax-deferred. Retirement income from a traditional IRA is taxed as ordinary income. 401(k)s and other qualified retirement plans may be rolled over into traditional IRAs when workers retire or change employers.

Wine, Women and Wealth – is a trademarked Five Rings Financial educational workshop designed to educate women about financial principals in a fun, relaxed environment.

WW&W – An abbreviation for Wine, Women and Wealth.

....

Definitions included in the glossary have been sourced from the following websites:
- https://www.investopedia.com/financial-term-dictionary
- https://en.wikipedia.org
- https://nerdwallet.com
- https://www.consolidatedcredit.org/personal-finances
- https://www.entreprenuer.com
- https://ca.reuters.com
- https://mkgenterprisescorp-client.com
- https://www.nationallife.com
- https://www.thestreet.com/personal-finance/

 Resources

Books

Included in this list are the books cited herein, as well as some of the great books we use in our team trainings and teaching our Money 101, Wine, Women & Wealth and Money, Mommy & Me workshops.

Chatzky, Jean Sherman. *Make Money, Not Excuses: Wake up, Take Charge, and Overcome Your Financial Fears Forever.* Three Rivers Press, 2008.

Chatzky, Jean Sherman. *The Difference: New Research Unlocks the 10 Secrets to Transforming Your Financial Future.* Crown Publishers, 2009.

Chatzky, Jean Sherman. *The Ten Commandments of Financial Happiness: Feel Richer with What You've Got.* Portfolio, 2004.

Freiberg, Jackie, and Kevin Freiberg. *Be a Person of Impact! 12 Strategies to Be the CEO of Your Future.* San Diego Consulting Group, Inc., 2015.

Freiberg, Jackie, and Kevin Freiberg. *Cause!: a Business Strategy for Standing out in a Sea of Sameness.* San Diego Consulting Group, Inc., 2015.

Harrison, K.L. *Grandma's Money Tree.* Clear Vision Press, 2017.

Judd, Kristen. *Own Your Future Journal: Your Habits Predict Your Future.* CreateSpace Independent Publishing Platform, 2017.

Kelly, Patrick. *Stress-Free Retirement.* Rubicon Publishing Inc., 2013.

Kelly, Patrick. *Tax-Free Retirement*. Trafford, 2007.

Kelly, Patrick. *The Retirement Miracle*. Bluewater Press, 2011.

Kemp, Robin Rascoe. *Protect and Grow Wealth: 5 Steps to Financial Freedom so You Can Have a Lifetime of Income, a Safety Net and Thrive!* Ignite Press, 2017.

Kobliner, Beth. *Make Your Kid a Money Genius (Even If You're Not): a Parents' Guide for Kids 3 to 23*. Simon & Schuster, 2017.

Lesser, Elizabeth. *Broken Open: How Difficult Times Can Help Us Grow*. Villard, 2005.

Madson, Jenifer. *A Financial Minute*. Clear Vision Press. 2006

Robbins, Anthony. *Money, Master the Game: 7 Simple Steps to Financial Freedom*. Simon & Schuster, 2016

Sincero, Jen. *You Are a Badass at Making Money Master the Mindset of Wealth*. Penguin Books, an Imprint of Penguin Random House LLC, 2018.

Resources

Websites

Here are some helpful and cited websites:

Five Rings Financial -
      https://www.fiveringsfinancial.com
      https://fiveringseducation.com

Wine Women and Wealth -
      https://www.winewomenwealth.org
      https://www.fiveringsfinancial.com/wine-women-wealth/

Terminology -
      https://www.investopedia.com/financial-term-dictionary-4769738

Calculators/Basic Financial Help -
      https://www.nerdwallet.com

Budgeting/Tracking/Basic Financial Help -
      https://www.mint.com

FIVE RINGS FINANCIAL
Vision Statement

IT IS THE DREAM of sharing the basics and fundamentals of a personal financial education with hundreds of thousands of Middle Americans – and helping them to apply what they have learned.

IT IS THE DREAM of offering a genuine and authentic career opportunity, part-time or full-time, and welcoming thousands of agents into the environment of our business family: Loving, Learning, Laughing and Working in harmony together.

IT IS THE DREAM of equipping every one of our teammates for a significant role by helping them discover the gifts and talents they possess.

IT IS THE DREAM of developing hundreds of financially independent leaders that expand our message and opportunity throughout hundreds of offices and communities.

IT IS THE DREAM of creating generational wealth for the partnership group and their families through profit-sharing and equity programs. It is the dream for Five Rings Financial to make a profound and positive impact in the lives of those willing to believe in and build their dream career in a dream company.

IT IS THE DREAM of a place where the hurting, the frustrated, the disillusioned and the confused can find love, acceptance, help, hope, guidance and encouragement. It is a home for people that need a second chance or a third chance or however many chances it takes.

Creating...
Opportunities • Income • Security • Wealth

FIVE RINGS FINANCIAL
Who we are...

Five Rings Financial, an Independent Marketing Organization (IMO), represents many of the world's largest financial services companies and is dedicated to serving the financial needs of individuals, families and businesses from all walks of life.

Our company is specifically designed to assist our clients in furthering their wealth-building education and in supporting clients who have reached a point of truly desiring to change or improve their financial position.

Our goal is to provide quality education to assist our clients in feeling empowered about making financial decisions and offer them recommendations that add value to their lives, families and businesses.

Although we are a national company in one of the world's most vital industries, our thousands of local independent associates and managers offer hometown value, service and education to each client, providing them the opportunity to achieve one of their most desired goals: financial independence.

In addition, Five Rings Financial offers a unique professional opportunity for individuals interested in pursuing a career in the financial services industry. By focusing on education and duplicable training systems, Five Rings Financial has created a model that refreshes the traditional industry approach and attracts producers who would rather "teach" than "sell".

Working primarily with Middle Americans, Five Rings Financial associates provide revolutionary strategies that create security and a safety net during life events and retirement.

From the Five Rings Financial Mission Statement

~147~